Stooges
AMONG US

EDITED BY LON & DEBRA DAVIS

FOREWORD BY LEONARD MALTIN

STOOGES AMONG US

©2008 LON AND DEBRA DAVIS (EDITORS)
AND RESPECTIVE AUTHORS.

PUBLISHED IN THE USA BY:
BEARMANOR MEDIA
P.O. BOX 71426
ALBANY, GEORGIA 31708
WWW.BEARMANORMEDIA.COM

LIBRARY OF CONGRESS CATALOGING-IN-PUBLICATION DATA:

Stooges among us / edited by Lon & Debra Davis ; foreword by Leonard Maltin.
    p. cm.
  ISBN 978-1-59393-300-5
  1. Three Stooges (Comedy team) 2. Three Stooges films--History and criticism.
I. Davis, Lon, 1959- II. Davis, Debra, 1956-

  PN1995.9.T5S79 2008
  791.4302'80922--dc22

                          2008023628

THE THREE STOOGES® IS A TRADEMARK OF C3 ENTERTAINMENT, INC.
THE THREE STOOGES® CHARACTERS, NAMES AND ALL RELATED INDICIA ARE
TRADEMARKS OF C3 ENTERTAINMENT, INC.
WWW.THREESTOOGES.COM

FRONT COVER PHOTOGRAPH: LARRY, MOE AND CURLY TAKE TO THE STREETS FOR A PUBLICITY SHOT;
HOLLYWOOD, CALIFORNIA, CIRCA 1934. *COURTESY OF C3 ENTERTAINMENT, INC.*

BACK COVER PHOTOGRAPH: LARRY, MOE (LEFT TO RIGHT, BACK SEAT) AND CURLY-JOE
(BARELY VISIBLE BEHIND WINDSHIELD) GREET THEIR FANS DURING A PARADE THROUGH
PITTSBURGH, PENNSYLVANIA, IN 1968. *COURTESY OF GARY LASSIN*

BOOK DESIGN AND LAYOUT BY VALERIE THOMPSON

TABLE OF CONTENTS

This book is dedicated to
Steve Libby . . .

. . . and all Stooge fans who never had
the chance to meet them.

"Stooges Among Us": ORIGINAL DRAWING BY COLE JOHNSON

FOREWORD
BY LEONARD MALTIN

In life, as in comedy, timing is everything.

I was lucky enough to be born into the first television generation, when local TV stations were a living museum of movie history. I got my daily dose of Laurel and Hardy and The Little Rascals, and a weekly trip into the world of animation hosted by Walt Disney himself.

Then, one day, a new attraction was added to the afternoon lineup on New York's Channel 11, WPIX. Being a full-time television junkie, I remember the introductory ad that appeared in *TV Guide* featuring one familiar face (local kiddie-show host "Officer" Joe Bolton) and three I'd never seen before. That was my first glimpse of Moe, Larry and Curly. I was eight years old.

It didn't take long for me to become a fan of The Three Stooges. I was among the millions of kids who made a beeline to my local movie theater when they appeared on the big screen — first in a compilation film called *Stop! Look! and Laugh!* and then in a brand-new feature called *Have Rocket, Will Travel.*

One could write off all these childhood memories as a simple case of pop-culture nostalgia. After all, a young person today has unprecedented access to vintage movies on DVD, while the Internet not only connects like-minded fans together but offers information that used to require endless hours of research at the public library.

But coming of age as I did in the late 1950s and 1960s I had one advantage over young people of the 21st century. I had the opportunity to have personal contact with many of the individuals who created the movies I cared about so much.

Growing up in New Jersey, I didn't have first-hand access to the stars of Hollywood, three thousand miles away, but I didn't do too badly. I wrote a get-well letter to Stan Laurel when he was recovering from a heart attack in 1964 and received a hand-written reply with a wonderful inscribed photo. I actually met Buster Keaton when he was shooting an experimental short-subject called *Film* on location in lower Manhattan.

And I carried on a long-range correspondence with Moe Howard.

You can only imagine how I felt when my first fan letter to Moe yielded a personal, hand-written reply that came in an envelope emblazoned with caricatures of Moe, Larry, and Curly-Joe — with an autographed photo inside.

That would have been enough, but I wrote back with specific questions from time to time, and he always responded. When I was working on a career article about that unsung comedian Charley Chase for my magazine *Film Fan Monthly* in 1968, Moe was kind enough to share his memories of working with Charley, who directed the Stooges in the late 1930s. "He played a guitar and sang very well," he wrote, "and we would all harmonize together real barbershop harmony, with Vernon Dent, who sang a beautiful tenor, and sometimes with Buddy Jamison, both of whom worked with Chaplin. They are all gone; what a sextet they must be having somewhere on high." Moe knew I was just a kid, but he treated me as if I were an adult, which meant the world to me.

It turns out that I wasn't the only one who experienced this generosity from Moe or his comedy cohorts. I suspect that he derived a great deal of pleasure from the outpouring of affection he received from a new generation of fans. We know for a fact that Larry Fine's later life was brightened by visits, phone calls and letters from fans around the world. Now, for the first time, Lon Davis has called upon a number of these fans and colleagues to share their memories of encounters with the Stooges. It's heartening to read about their experiences and realize how lucky we all were.

A child of the 21st century can still fall under the spell of silent comedy and the golden age of talkie two-reel comedies, especially if he or she has a parent who wants to pass on a love for these films. But a precocious twelve-year-old can't become a pen-pal with one of their legendary stars, or stumble onto them on a local television show one afternoon. I did, and so did most of the others who contributed to this book, and I daresay we'll never forget it.

LEONARD MALTIN, THE WELL-KNOWN CRITIC AND FILM HISTORIAN, REGULARLY APPEARS ON THE POPULAR SYNDICATED TELEVISION SHOW, *ENTERTAINMENT TONIGHT*, AND IS THE EDITOR OF THE #1 BEST-SELLER, *LEONARD MALTIN'S MOVIE GUIDE*. LEONARD'S BACKGROUND WITH THE THREE STOOGES HAS BEEN AN IMPRESSIVE ONE. HE COMPILED THEIR FIRST FILMOGRAPHY FOR A 1968 ARTICLE IN HIS MAGAZINE, *FILM FAN MONTHLY*. HE LATER EXPANDED THIS INTO A CHAPTER FOR HIS 1970 BOOK, *MOVIE COMEDY TEAMS*, AND WROTE FURTHER ABOUT THE GROUP IN *THE GREAT MOVIE SHORTS* (1972) AND *THE GREAT MOVIE COMEDIANS* (1978). HE ALSO CO-PRODUCED AND WROTE A HOME VIDEO DOCUMENTARY, *THE LOST STOOGES*, IN 1990.

Introduction

The Three Stooges.

If you look up the word "Comedy" in the dictionary, you'll literally see their picture.* The Stooges deserve to be the symbol of laughter. They created more than their fair share of it in a career that encompassed vaudeville, two-reelers, features, cartoons, television and personal appearances. Theirs is an extraordinary comic legacy.

By the early 1970s the Three Stooges (in their various incarnations) had ceased to exist as a show business act. Two of the most talented members of the legendary team — Curly and Shemp Howard — were long dead. But four authentic Stooges still remained: Moe Howard, Larry Fine, Joe Besser and Joe DeRita. As their younger images cavorted on television sets around the country, the actual flesh-and-blood men were dealing with the all-too-common effects of aging. Larry Fine had suffered a major stroke and was convalescing at an industry-supported retirement facility. Joe Besser spent his days caring for his ailing wife. Joe DeRita's escalating weight was taking its toll on his small frame. And Moe Howard, by far the most visible and active of the surviving funnymen, suffered from hearing loss. They all lived in the Los Angeles area and in the Joes' case, at least, were listed in the local telephone directory. Each of these men had given their professional lives to make the world laugh. It was time for their fans to say "thank you."

---

* Okay, maybe not the dictionary, but certainly in the 1968 *World Book* Encyclopedia, volume Ci to Cz; pg. 700.

And we did: through letters, cards, calls and personal visits. Most of the Stooges' acolytes were teenaged males, high school students who preferred old movies to current ones; vaudeville ditties to the latest rock song. Now a bunch of middle-aged businessmen, writers, radio hosts, accountants, lawyers, scientists, animators, producers, actors, husbands and fathers, we realize in retrospect just how fortunate we were to have known our childhood idols. We are also pleased to have this chance to share our experiences, photographs and interviews — most of which are being seen in print for the first time.

A number of special guests are contributing their memories in this book. Rose Marie (Sally of *The Dick Van Dyke Show*) reveals how Jerry Howard actually became known as "Curley." Diana Serra Cary (the former silent film star "Baby Peggy") remembers seeing Ted Healy and His Stooges in vaudeville in 1928. Adam West (star of the classic *Batman* television series) describes his experience of co-starring with the Stooges in their final theatrical feature, *The Outlaws Is Coming!* And *Laugh-In* announcer Gary Owens details his successful quest to get the Stooges their richly deserved star on the Hollywood Walk of Fame.

Family members are opening up about their famous relatives within these pages: Joan Howard Maurer shares a poignant piece on her beloved father, Moe; Eric Lamond (Larry's eldest grandson) humorously tells of his stint as a technician on the Stooges' cartoon series; and Sandie Howard relates a warm tribute to her grandfather Shemp. Another special contributor (and family member) is Gary Lassin, President of the Three Stooges Fan Club and founder of the Stoogeum in Spring House, Pennsylvania.

And finally, we are honored by the involvement of Leonard Maltin, the renowned movie critic and historian. Mr. Maltin was a pioneer in the documentation of the Stooges' careers.

The essays in this book have been written for one basic reason. Each of us want to share with you, the reader, what it was like to live in a world where there really were Stooges Among Us.

FINE MEMORIES

BY LON DAVIS

During the Psychedelic Sixties parents everywhere were trying to keep their kids away from drugs. My father, on the other hand, was trying to keep me away from the Three Stooges. They were, he believed, "a bad influence." What did he think I was going to do — watch one of their shorts and then uncontrollably throw pies and jab neighbor kids in the eyes?

Whatever his reasoning, I chose to ignore the edict. On most every weekday afternoon I'd rush home from grade school to watch the Stooges on New York's WPIX-Channel 11 in the basement-den of a friend's house.* I never laughed so hard in my life! Neither, for that matter, did the other boys watching the black and white films with me. At the show's conclusion — as though on a sugar high — we'd run around the room imitating Curly's "Woo-Woo-Woo" and Shemp's "Heep-Heep-Heep," poking and slapping one other, and throwing pillows as though they were pies.

Okay — so maybe Dad had a point.

Over the next few years I spent a healthy percentage of my lawn-mowing money on Stooge-related merchandise: Gold Key comic books, Fleer bubble gum cards, 8mm silent abridgments of the Columbia two-reelers. In a studious vein, I all but memorized the Stooge filmography in Leonard Maltin's seminal book, *Movie Comedy Teams*.

---

* New York-based fans fondly recall Officer Joe Bolton, who hosted the Three Stooges comedies each weekday afternoon at 4:00. Just which "third Stooge" would be featured was determined by the day of the week: Curly was relegated to Monday and Thursday; Shemp to Tuesday and Friday; and Joe Besser to Wednesday.

Meeting an Old Friend

I liked all of the Stooges, of course, but my favorite was Larry Fine, the one with the bushy hair surrounding his balding head. He is sometimes referred to as "The Stooge in the Middle," since he was usually caught in the crossfire between Moe and Curly. Coming to Curly's rescue during one of Moe's tirades, Larry would say, "Hey, leave him alone," and be rewarded with a slap in the face for his troubles.

Larry spent his final years as a resident of the Motion Picture Country House in Woodland Hills, a Los Angeles suburb in the West San Fernando Valley. Established in 1942, the MPCH is an industry-supported facility that caters to the medical and financial needs of its long-time members. "We take care of our own" is the Fund's accurate slogan.

One grateful recipient of this care was my great-uncle, Ted Edlin, who had been a bit player and makeup artist for over fifty years. My family and I visited Uncle Ted at the Motion Picture Home whenever we were in Southern California, and on one particular occasion — Thanksgiving Weekend of 1973 — I decided to do some further investigation on my own.

The facility consists of individual cottages, a building known as the Lodge, and a state-of-the-art hospital. Since I was a particularly outgoing fourteen-year-old, I dropped in unannounced on any resident whose door was open. In that informal manner I met someone from virtually every facet of the motion picture industry. There were retired photographers and makeup artists, featured players and character actors, secretaries and technicians. Some of the notable residents (at one time or another) have included Bud Abbott, G.M. "Broncho Billy" Anderson, Mary Astor, Chester Conklin, Wendell Corey, Billie Dove, Max Fleischer, Hattie McDaniel, Mack Sennett, Johnny Weissmuller — and, of course, an original Stooge or two.

I asked the receptionist at the front desk in the Lodge if I could meet Larry Fine. She promptly went to his door and knocked on it.

"Come in," I heard him call out.

When she opened the door, I could see that he was seated in a brown leather chair, watching television.

Larry as a doughboy in *Gents Without Cents* (Columbia Pictures, 1944).
COURTESY OF C3 ENTERTAINMENT, INC.

"Larry," I said (it never occurred to me to call him "Mr. Fine"), "would you mind if I came in for a few minutes?"

"You might as well," he said, turning off the evening news with a remote control, "there's nothing good on anyway."

I was struck by how much Larry had changed since his days in the public eye. A major contributor to this was the debilitating stroke he had suffered three years earlier. As a result of this, his once-rapid delivery had been slowed and his words were slurred. And at seventy-one, he was nine years older than the reference books alleged. He was shorter than I expected also: like Moe, Larry was only five-feet-four-inches tall. Certainly the biggest surprise of all was his hair. Once an unmanageable bush, it was now shorn, graying, and combed back in a dignified manner. But despite the ravages of time and illness, it was still Larry — still the same man whose face belonged with the other Stooges on the comedy version of Mount Rushmore.

I took a mental picture of my surroundings. The room had a double bed upon which rested a few stuffed animals. Staring down from the walls were some black and white glossies and caricatures of Larry in his prime. His long writing desk was littered with fan mail. Also on his desk was a framed photograph dating back to his earliest days in vaudeville. Larry was recognizable as a diminutive teenager in the group shot. He noticed that I was looking at the faded picture.

"Would you believe that that is me — ?"

"When you were part of Gus Edwards' Newsboy Sextet in 1915," I said with some authority.

Larry seemed taken aback. "Yeah," he said.

I explained that I had made a study of American vaudeville and was also a collector of early film comedies. Recently I had begun showing my 16mm prints at high schools and colleges in the Phoenix area. The students, I told him, laughed moderately at Laurel and Hardy, W.C. Fields, Charlie Chaplin and the Keystone Cops, but when I showed the 1940 Stooge two-reeler, *Boobs in Arms*, teachers from adjoining classrooms complained that the loud laughter boomed through the walls.

Larry seemed to like the idea that the formally uneducated Stooges were disrupting the Hallowed Halls of Academia.

Despite our fifty-seven-year age difference, Larry and I discovered that we had more in common than just a mutual interest in comedy. We were both born in the eastern part of the United States and now lived in the west; we were both animal lovers; we both enjoyed staying awake until all hours; and neither one of us had a particularly keen attention span when it came to serious matters.

Suddenly there came a loud buzzing from his nightstand intercom. He reached over and flipped a switch. "Yeah?" he said.

"Mr. Fine," a female voice intoned, "you have a caller on line three."

"Okay."

I assisted him into his wheelchair and took him down a corridor toward a communal telephone. When he was poised to lift the receiver, I offered my goodbyes.

Larry touched me on the arm. "You don't really have to go, do you?"

"I guess not," I answered.

"Let me just take this call," he said, "then we can *really* talk."

And talk we did: sometimes in his room, occasionally through letters, but mostly during my weekly telephone calls to him. All of this was my concerted effort to learn as much as possible about Larry in the brief time he had left. He told me about his childhood, about his years in vaudeville, about his wife and family — and, of course, he talked about his fellow Stooges.

Larry's Early Years

He was born Louis Feinberg at 606 South Third Street in Philadelphia, Pennsylvania, on October 5, 1902. As a toddler, he sustained an injury that would indirectly lead to his career in show business. His father was looking after him one day as he attended to some projects in his watch repair and jewelry shop. While his back was turned, his infant son reached for the bottle of acid used to test gold. Before Larry could drink from it, Mr. Feinberg knocked the bottle out of his hand, inadvertently spilling acid on the baby's arm. The burn was severe, and required a skin graft. Doctors feared that it would even impede his growth. It was therefore recommended that he take up violin lessons at the earliest possible date, since the action of moving the bow back and forth might strengthen his arm and hand muscles. Larry did as he was told, and developed a life-long love of music.

Truth to tell, he wasn't an especially gifted violinist, but what talent he did have allowed him to find steady work in small-time vaudeville, beginning at the age of thirteen. He later changed his name to "Fine" and hit the big time with an act he developed called "At the Crossroads," featuring the Haney Sisters. They toured the RKO, Orpheum, Keith-Orpheum and Delmar vaudeville circuits between 1921 and 1925. The Haney Sisters and Fine eventually dissolved as an act, but not so Larry's relationship with Mabel Haney. They were in love, and not even their differing religions (he was Jewish; she was Roman Catholic) could keep them apart. In 1926 Larry and Mabel were married. They had two children, a daughter named Phyllis and a son named Johnny.

TED HEALY

The man who made the word "stooge" a vaudeville staple was born Charles Earnest Lee Nash on October 1, 1896, in Kaufman, Texas. After studying business for over a decade, he changed his plans and became a stand-up comic. His act consisted of impressions of such well-known personalities as Ed Wynn, Eddie Cantor and Al Jolson. Encouraged by his success, Nash dropped the imitations and changed his name to Ted Healy. Standing over six feet tall and sporting a comically crushed hat, Healy developed a solid reputation as a performer, earning as much as $8,500 a week.

In 1922 Healy teamed with a young woman named Betty Brown, who later became his partner offstage as well as on. Two years later he approached his boyhood pal Moe Howard about filling in as a "stooge" (a vaudeville term used to describe a comedian's assistant), and Moe agreed to do so for "a couple of days."

Those couple of days stretched into nine years.

Moe's older brother Shemp joined in as well and the act became known variously as Ted Healy and his Stooges, "Racketeers" or "Southern Gentlemen." Not that there was anything gentlemanly about their onstage exploits. Healy knocked Moe and Shemp around the stage while the audience roared.

Healy and the Howard Brothers first saw Larry Fine in 1925 at Chicago's Rainbo Gardens nightclub and felt that he might make a

Ted Healy and His Stooges recreate their vaudeville act (without the benefit of a live audience) in the 1933 Metro-Goldwyn-Mayer short, *Plane Nuts*.
COURTESY OF THE COLE JOHNSON SLAPSTICK ARCHIVE

good addition to their act. Moe later said that he and Healy approached Larry backstage and offered him the job, provided that he left his violin at home. Larry agreed to this and was soon standing alongside Moe and Shemp, awaiting Healy's stinging triple-slap.

The mistreatment was not limited to the stage. Healy paid his subordinates a meager wage and slugged them when alcohol got the better of him, which was often. As he explained to a reporter at the time: "a stooge comes in handy when you feel like throwing something at somebody. Whenever I'm in doubt or feel mixed up, I always hit the nearest stooge. Makes me feel better."

From time to time, the Stooges would quit, but their persuasive straight-man managed to manipulate them into returning. Shemp, though, had suffered enough indignities at Healy's hand and chose to try his luck in the movies instead. He was making a name for himself in two-reelers at about the same time that Healy and his Stooges were doing some guest shots for Fox and MGM. The newest member of the team by then was Jerome Howard, better known as "Curly."

As Healy's alcoholism escalated, so too did the nature of his abuse. The Stooges finally walked out on their mentor one day in 1933 and never looked back. They went on to achieve cinematic immortality while Ted Healy slowly faded into obscurity.

GROWN MEN IN SHORTS

Moe, Larry and Curly (now billed simply as The Three Stooges) signed with the Columbia short-subjects department on Gower Street in Hollywood. This was to be their professional home for twenty-four consecutive years. In 190 two-reelers the Stooges were always fish out of water, wreaking havoc wherever they went. The ruffians destroyed more than one high society soiree with their pie throwing and general incompetence. This "upsetting of dignity" — as Moe categorized it — greatly appealed to Depression-era audiences.

Over the years the Stooges tackled such diverse topics as World War II, politics, married life, babysitting and bullfighting. They routinely satirized such genres as the western, the historical epic, gothic horror and science fiction films. Moe, Larry and Curly are not icons today because of their storylines, however, but because of their heavy reliance on physical comedy. In a sense, the Stooges were carrying on the rich tradition established by producer Mack Sennett in the silent era. And indeed, a number of notable silent comedy veterans participated in the making of the Stooges' films, including directors Del Lord and Charley Chase, frequent co-stars Vernon Dent, Bud Jamison, Kenneth MacDonald, and gagmen Felix Adler and Clyde Bruckman.

Moe, Curly and Larry in a scene from *Playing the Ponies* (Columbia Pictures, 1937). COURTESY OF C3 ENTERTAINMENT, INC.

Another important element of the humor stems from the use of sound effects. When Moe slapped Larry, for instance, the sound of a whiplash accentuated the action. If he poked Shemp in the eyes, a plunk of a violin string is heard. And if he punched Curly in the stomach, you knew you were going to hear the thud of a bass drum. Sound also played a vital role in the Stooges' vaudeville-style dialogue:

SHEMP (making a discovery): "Eureka!"

MOE: "*You* don't smell so good either."

Critics, of course, held their noses at this low form of comedy, but the public — particularly in small towns — couldn't get enough of it. As one Utah exhibitor wrote in a trade journal in 1937: "This trio of comedians are the hit of the show. They are nine-tenths of my box-office appeal for the kids. You can have your Marx Brothers and your Laurel and Hardy, but give me just one feature-length Stooge picture and I'll be out of the red for a good while. Thank you Curly, Larry and Moe. You are tops with me."

Although the shorts were consistent moneymakers for Columbia, the studio treated the Stooges rather shabbily. The team initially split $1,500 for each short they made, which amounted to a yearly sum of approximately $10,000. This figure was not bad for three high-school dropouts during the Depression, but it was paltry for three hard-working movie stars. Moe was fearful that Columbia's tyrannical chief, Harry Cohn, would drop their option if he asked for more money, so he simply remained silent at contract negotiation time. This frustrated Larry, who was also unhappy that Columbia limited the team to short subjects.

"We could have been just as big as the Marx Brothers if they had just put us in features," he once said to me.

After Columbia disbanded its shorts department, the Stooges received their walking papers. They had made millions for the studio and had outperformed every comedy team in history in terms of productivity. One of their earliest two-reelers, *Men in Black*, was even nominated for an Academy Award. Yet their salary in 1958 wasn't that much more than it had been in 1934. They had made their real money by performing live in theaters across the United States. Now Moe and Larry seemed to be facing the end of the line. They were getting on in years and their brand of slapstick comedy was dismissed as anachronistic. With no bookings on the horizon, they considered breaking up the act for good. Moe decided to take a stab at the solo acting career he had abandoned some forty years earlier.

MOE

With his tight-lipped grimace, his baggy eyes and his spittoon haircut, Moe Howard has emerged as one of comedy's most recognizable straight men. Like Oliver Hardy, Moe's character felt intellectually superior to those around him, when in fact, he was quite possibly the dumbest guy in the room. His cocksure approach always seemed to backfire and it was he, not his knuckleheaded partners, who received the bulk of the resulting injuries.

In his private life, Moe always presented himself as a gentleman, with his hair neatly slicked back. COURTESY OF C3 ENTERTAINMENT, INC.

The name "Moe" derived from his real name — Moses. He was born in Brooklyn, New York, on June 19, 1897, the fourth of five sons of Lithuanian immigrants Solomon and Jennie Horwitz. As young boys, Moe, Shemp and four-year-old Jerome occasionally performed together in basement productions of neighborhood shows. Moe, whose other interests included sports and girls, was by all accounts a healthy, well-adjusted youth. His mother, however, had always wanted a daughter, and she loved to fuss over her son's long brown curls. Moe grew tired of this treatment and one day took a pair of scissors to his hair, giving himself the bowl-cut that would later become his trademark.

His first movie appearances were in 1909 when he volunteered his services at the Vitagraph Studio, located several miles from his home in Brooklyn. Twelve-year-old Moe was an errand boy who occasionally appeared on camera as a bit player. He further demonstrated his independence by running away from home to join a Mississippi riverboat show. The stage-struck youth gained invaluable experience on the road when he performed in stock company productions of both comedies and melodramas. In 1921 he and Shemp went into vaudeville together, calling themselves "Howard and Howard." Appearing last on many a small-time bill, their "blackface" act was so bad that it invariably cleared the theatre to make way for the next rowdy audience.

At the end of their volatile nine-year association with Ted Healy, Moe assumed Healy's role as the physically punishing boss of Larry and Curly. He became the team's undisputed leader, offscreen as well as on.

A solemn, intense individual, Moe Howard lived to work. It was his driving spirit, in fact, that kept the team going in the face of changing times and death. Not that he was unfeeling, not at all. He was grieved by the loss of his brothers, and according to Larry, he even wept uncontrollably upon hearing of Ted Healy's untimely passing in 1937. Whether he wanted to admit it or not, Moe was actually a softie in real life. He was a worshipful husband to his wife, Helen, and a devoted father to their two children, Joan and Paul.

In their films, Moe was always addressing Larry as "chowderhead," "frizzletop," "lamebrain," or "nitwit." In real life, he was far more explicit with his insults, particularly if Larry was late to an engagement — which was often. He was even known to resort to a more direct form of physical remonstration. Moe was an artist with his hands ("He could've been a pickpocket," Larry liked to say) and he could execute a perfect "stiff-fingered" slap, meaning that he could make contact with his partners' faces without inflicting pain. When Larry sauntered onto the stage — late again — Moe signaled to his tardy subordinate that he was wearing a ring on his slapping hand. This meant Larry was in for some hard hits. But, by this point in his career, he had been struck in the face so many times he had a permanent callus on his cheek. He barely felt it.

Even in retirement, Larry felt intimidated by the mop-topped bully. I witnessed this firsthand on one memorable occasion.

"Let's give Moe a call today," I said during one of my rare in-person visits.

Larry wasn't overly enthusiastic about the idea, but he indulged me anyway. I wheeled him to a lobby pay phone and he inserted the necessary coins. Moe's wife Helen answered and Larry talked to her for a few minutes. Mrs. Howard then turned the call over to her husband. Larry went through the typical amenities and then, with barely an introduction, he handed me the receiver.

Moe sounded tired and clearly did not appreciate having his Sunday afternoon interrupted. He listened politely, however, while I babbled on about how much I loved the Stooges. I had recently seen him demonstrating the art of pie throwing on Mike Douglas's television talk show, and his aim — even at the age of seventy-six — was as precise as ever. *No one*, I told him admiringly, had ever thrown a pie with more finesse than Moe Howard.

He agreed: "Someone at Columbia once told me that I saved the studio thousands upon thousands of dollars in retakes by hitting my mark the first time out."

I then asked how his autobiography was progressing.

"Slow," he admitted.

"Just think," I said, "when it's done, there'll be *three* books on the Three Stooges."

"Whaddya mean, three?" he asked suspiciously.

"Well," I explained, "Larry's book came out last year; then there's yours, and now Larry's coming out with another one . . ."

"Since *when?*" His tone was suddenly menacing. I looked up and saw that Larry's face was pale.

"Moe's not supposed to know about my new book," he whispered.

(I later discovered that Larry's first memoir — a badly written mishmash called *Stroke of Luck* — had rankled Moe. He was, after all, the team's spokesman, and *he* wanted to be the first Stooge to present a written record of their history. Larry knew this, but went ahead and made a deal with a new writer to begin work on a second book. And now I had, as the saying goes, "let the cat out of the bag.")

I tried to clean up the mess I'd made by telling Moe that I must have been mistaken: there was no book, no book at all — I was just a dumb kid; I didn't know what I was talking about. I then hurriedly signed off, saying that it had been a real pleasure talking to him, and hung up the receiver.

"Larry," I said apologetically, "I'm sorry I got you into trouble with Moe. I'd like to shoot myself. You don't have a gun, do you?"

"No," he replied stone-faced, "but I can borrow one."

CURLY

Moe may have been the leader of the team, but Curly most definitely marched to the beat of his own drummer. Like Harpo Marx, this comic was one of the screen's true surrealists. Curly was a child in a man's body: a bizarre, manic, noise-making machine. Over the years, his high-pitched voice and unique laugh ("N'yuk, n'yuk, n'yuk") have been widely imitated, but never equaled. He was, without question, the most popular of the Stooges — and he knew it.

"Curly used to say to Moe and me, 'I don't need you guys; I'm just keeping you afloat.'" Larry shook his head at that memory.

To understand the basis of Curly's nature, one needs to examine his painful past. He was born Jerome Lester Horwitz on October 22, 1903, in Brooklyn, New York. The youngest of the future Howard brothers, Jerome (or "Babe" as he was known to family) preferred the extracurricular activities of sports and music to his studies in the classroom. He was also something of a ladies' man, and married while still in his teens. His mother protested this union, however, and six months later she had the marriage annulled.

Curly was very self-conscious of his trademark buzz-cut and therefore favored hats. COURTESY OF C3 ENTERTAINMENT, INC.

In 1928 Jerome made his debut as a professional entertainer, performing a comic routine as a conductor for a band. Although it may seem difficult to imagine, he was considered quite handsome at that time in his life. He had, by his own description, "beautiful wavy hair and a waxed mustache." But these adornments of vanity had to go when he was enlisted as a Stooge in 1932. Nicknamed "Curley," the twenty-nine-year-old came to resemble — in Moe's words — "a dirty tennis ball."

Curly (as the name was ultimately spelled) was brilliantly funny when in character, and his involvement with the team was vital to their emerging success. But beneath the comic mask was a deeply self-conscious individual. He felt (accurately) that his new look had robbed him of his sex appeal. To hide his childish buzz-cut in public, he almost always wore a hat. And to help him overcome his shyness, he drank to excess.

Alcohol also served as a balm for a lingering injury he had suffered when he was a boy. While cleaning a rifle he accidentally shot himself in the ankle. As he never properly treated the wound, it left him with a permanent limp. By exaggerating his gait, he developed the peculiar walk that became an important weapon in his comic arsenal.

Success would bring more pain than pleasure to this favored Stooge. Completely unable to handle money, he spent every cent he had on sumptuous homes, cars, prize-winning boxer dogs, and women — especially women. Curly married four times, and all of these marriages but one ended poorly. One of his wives claimed in court that he used vile language, abused her physically and verbally, and put out his cigars in the kitchen sink.

He also overate, which caused his weight to balloon. Diagnosed with extreme hypertension and a retinal hemorrhage, Curly became a ticking time bomb.

"I think Curly had a small stroke in 1945 and never told us," Larry said.

After this, the childlike comic became slowed, his timing ruined. (Watching his lethargic performances in shorts made during that period can be heartbreaking.) Then, during the filming of his ninety-seventh Stooge short in 1946, he suffered a major stroke. Moe and Larry had to finish the film without him.

After three failed marriages, Curly found the perfect spouse in Valerie Newman. The couple had a daughter, Janie, who brightened Curly's life considerably during these trying times. When Valerie was no longer able to provide the constant care that her husband required, she admitted him to the Motion Picture Country Home; he was later moved to a private sanitarium in San Gabriel. He died there on January 18, 1952.

Curly Howard was only forty-eight years old.

SHEMP

Curly's incapacitation brought Shemp back into the fold. He became a Stooge again in 1947 and went on to star in seventy-seven shorts over the next eight years. Shemp's long greasy black hair and strong family resemblance to Moe failed to offer the contrast that Curly had so effortlessly provided. But Shemp had a style all his own, complete with exaggerated mugging and hilarious double-takes. His inspired improvisations infused the Stooges' shorts with a vitality that had been sadly lacking in the final Curly offerings.

A surprisingly handsome portrait of the so-called "Ugliest Man in Hollywood." COURTESY OF C3 ENTERTAINMENT, INC.

"Shemp had a way of saying something ridiculous with a completely straight face," Larry told me with a grin. "And he knew he could crack you up."

This Stooge's Stooge was given the Hebrew name of Schmool when he was born in Brooklyn, New York, on March 17, 1895. Schmool became anglized to Samuel, and then shortened to Sam. But when his mother attempted to pronounce "Sam" in her thick Lithuanian accent, it came out sounding like "Shemp."

As he matured, he developed a character of a tough-talking wiseguy, although the real Shemp Howard was anything but that in real life. He was a deeply sensitive individual, a chronic bed wetter, and a notorious hypochondriac. He also had a host of phobias, including hotels and airplanes. Hotels were especially challenging for him since he was convinced they were full of bedbugs. He would not even set foot into a hotel room until his wife Gertrude (or "Babe") had fully inspected it for insects. But perhaps his greatest fear was of automobiles. As a boy he had been involved in a minor collision and never emotionally recovered from the trauma. For the rest of his life he refused to learn to drive — even being a passenger filled him with dread.

Ironically, Shemp's life ended in the backseat of a car. One November evening in 1955 he and his friend Al Winston were traveling in a cab to Shemp's North Hollywood home. The two men had just attended a boxing match and they were animatedly discussing the fight. Suddenly, Shemp slumped onto Winston's lap, his lit cigar still burning in his hand.

He had died of a cerebral hemorrhage at the age of sixty.

Shemp Howard's legacy lives on. His colleagues praise him for his kindness, his professionalism, and his comic ability. The late Bowery Boy Huntz Hall told me that Shemp had been his greatest influence, the man after whom he patterned his own screen image. Connoisseurs (or "common sewers," as Larry might say) regularly opine that Shemp was the most talented member of the group. He was certainly one of the most innovative comics in the history of slapstick.

Consider this actual scenario that occurred sometime in the late twenties. While waiting to go onstage, Shemp and Larry passed the time by playing cards. This particular game was anything but relaxing and the tension between the two men became palpable. Without warning, Shemp reached across the table and gave his card-partner a two-fingered poke in the eyes. Tears streamed down Larry's face as he called Shemp a "son of a bitch." Moe, meanwhile, had witnessed this incident and supposedly laughed so hard that he fell through a glass door.

So began the dreaded "eye jab," the bit that more than anything caused a generation of parents to revile the Stooges.

I was fascinated by this dangerous-looking stunt and asked Larry to show me how it was done. He was sitting across from me at the time, and he reached over and executed a perfectly aimed jab to my brow bone — *BINK.*

I instantly covered my eyes and said, "I can't see, I can't *see*!"

"How come?" Larry asked, alarmed.

I looked straight at him and said in my best Curly imitation, "I got my eyes closed."

Recognizing this exchange from any one of a dozen shorts, Larry gave me a disgusted look. Over my raucous laughter, I heard him mutter something that sounded suspiciously like, "Son of a bitch."

JOE BESSER

With Shemp now gone, Moe and Larry considered continuing on as "The Two Stooges," but their director Jules White had a replacement in mind — a chubby, balding comic named Joe Besser. A veteran in virtually every arena of show business, Besser had made a career out of playing a whining child. At times his portrayal was so literal that he donned a Buster Brown suit, skipped around the stage and took playful swipes at his co-stars. If anyone should dare strike him back — however lightly — he would wave his hands in the air and squeal, "Ow! That huuuuuuuuuuurrts!"

This, in many ways, reflected the man's true nature, as Besser hated being hit. He was starring in his own series of shorts for Columbia when he was pressured to become a member of the world's most physical comedy team. Fearing potential injury, he insisted that his contract stipulate that he not be struck or harmed in any way during the making of the shorts.

Joe, Larry and Moe seemed to have cooked up something appetizing in the Besser/Stooge entry, *Rusty Romeos* (Columbia Pictures, 1957).
COURTESY OF C3 ENTERTAINMENT, INC.

Larry told him, "Don't worry. If you don't want Moe to hit you, I'll take all the belts."

Born in St. Louis, Missouri, on August 12, 1907, Joe Besser followed his brother Manny into vaudeville. Joe's first big break came in 1933 when he was cast in the long-running Broadway show *Sons of Fun* starring the team of Olsen and Johnson. Besser went on to star on radio with Milton Berle and Jack Benny, on television with Abbott & Costello and Joey Bishop and in movies with Bing Crosby and Jerry Lewis. But it was his stint as a Stooge from 1956-1958 that earned him lasting recognition.

In 1974 I conducted the first of several revealing telephone interviews with Joe Besser. All but retired by this time, the sixty-seven-year-old comedian lived a quiet existence with his wife Erna in a modest house in North Hollywood. It was almost distracting to hear Joe's voice over the phone, since he sounded exactly as he had in the shorts. Once in the middle of a call, my brother Chris, not realizing I was in the middle of a conversation with the famous comedian, picked up an extension and began dialing. The clicking sound annoyed Joe terribly, and he yelled his signature phrase, "NOT SO LOOOOOUUUUUUUD!" into the receiver. Chris hung up immediately. In all seriousness, he later said to me: "That guy you were talking to does a *really good* Joe Besser."

Joe was delighted at being remembered and loved talking about his career, but was somewhat vague about his tenure with the Stooges. When I gently pressed him for details on a given scene, he told me that he couldn't remember it, and what's more, he had never even seen any of the sixteen films in which he was featured.

I began to suspect that Joe didn't care for Moe and Larry. Not that he ever spoke against his former partners ("I love everybody," was his oft-repeated line), but he preferred to keep his business and personal lives separate. This became clear to me when I asked him if he would like to meet Larry and me for lunch at the Motion Picture Home. He muttered something about being "too busy," and the subject was dropped.

In fact, Joe did have some lingering hurt feelings regarding the way he had been "dumped" by Larry and Moe. It must have been quite obvious to these slapstick masters that as talented a comedian as Besser was, he simply wasn't Stooge material. As for Joe, he may not have cared for their two-fisted comedy, but a job was a job, and he enjoyed the paycheck. The official reason given for his departure was that his wife was ill and that he needed to care for her.

The "Third Stooge" position was about to be filled one last time.

JOE DeRITA

To fit into the act, this roly-poly comic shaved his head and called himself "Curly-Joe." The resemblance to his famous predecessor ends there. Joe DeRita's character was more grounded in reality than Curly, but his understated humor and relaxed delivery blended seamlessly with his aging partners.

Larry, Moe and Joe on one of their many visits to the Children's Hospital of Los Angeles, circa 1968. COURTESY OF C3 ENTERTAINMENT, INC.

He was born Joseph Wardell on July 12, 1909, in Philadelphia, Pennsylvania. The only member of the celebrated team to come from a theatrical family, Joe performed in vaudeville from the time he was seven years old. He was also the only Stooge who was not of the Jewish faith.

Joining the team in 1958 proved fortuitous indeed for DeRita as he was just in time to reap the benefits of the Stooges' last great wave of popularity. A significant factor in this renaissance was the new slant used to market the trio. Now under the management of Moe's son-in-law Norman Maurer, the Stooges became even more overtly geared toward children. And to make their comedy more acceptable to parents, the violent slapstick of the earlier shorts all but disappeared. These kinder, gentler Stooges may not have been as funny as their younger selves, but they were infinitely more successful. Throughout the sixties Moe, Larry and Curly-Joe performed their toned-down routines at children's hospitals and orphanages, always arriving with a carload of gifts on Christmas morning.

Moe and Larry did not receive a cent in residuals from the televised showing of their old two-reelers, but the renewed fame did bring about other opportunities. There were record-breaking personal appearances; there were a handful of profitable feature films; there was a television cartoon series; there was a line of comic books, record albums, toys, bubblegum cards — the merchandising was endless. Comedy III, the company formed in 1960 to handle their licensing, reported $137,619 in revenues, almost ten times their annual salary during their prime years at Columbia. This figure would remain steady for at least five years.

For the Stooges, these were the best of times.

THE WORST OF TIMES

Nineteen sixty-five saw the release of the team's last feature, a western satire called *The Outlaws Is Coming!* After this modest hit, the market for children's films dried up and the Stooges began their slow fade to black.

Moe could certainly afford to retire — not that he ever would, of course. By contrast, Larry had little more than bruises to show for all the years he had spent as a human punching bag.

"Where did all the money go?" I asked him.

"I just pissed it away," he said with a shrug.

By that he meant he had lost some of it by betting on baseball games and horse races. There were also hotel bills to be paid; Larry and Mabel had a luxury suite at the Knickerbocker in Hollywood. Mabel Fine was not in the least domestic, and Larry saw to it that she never had to cook or do housework. It seemed he couldn't do enough for his wife of forty years. He treated her like a queen, running out at three in the morning for her favorite Chinese food and lavishing her with expensive jewelry. Mabel even insisted that Larry wear a chauffeur's cap while driving her around in their four-door Lincoln automobile. Some have speculated that Larry was trying to compensate for the many casual affairs he had, but I saw the look in his eyes when he talked about Mabel. This was a man in love.

During Memorial Day weekend of 1967, he and the boys were making one of their final personal appearances. Larry placed a call to his wife, but Mabel told him she couldn't talk just then. She explained that she was washing her hair and asked that he call her back in a few minutes. Larry hung up, only to hear the phone ring a short time later. His daughter, Phyllis, was on the end of the line.

"Dad," she said, "Mother is dead."

Mabel's death from a heart attack had been that sudden. Larry never fully recovered from the shock of this news, nor from the magnitude of his loss. He also continued to mourn his son, Johnny, who had died in a car accident in 1961.

In 1969 Moe, Larry, Joe and Norman Maurer pooled their funds to film an hour-long television pilot, ultimately released to the home movie market as *Kook's Tour*. Part travelogue and part situation comedy, the premise had the team retiring from show business and setting out together on a tour of the United States. The shoot was doomed from the outset, and although everyone involved did his best, it was clear that the Stooges had finally reached the end of their very long road.

THE LIFE OF THE PARTY

In January of 1970 Larry was felled by a massive stroke. At first paralyzed and unable to speak, he underwent intensive physical therapy. Slowly but surely, he regained some of his motor skills, although he would be confined to a wheelchair for the remainder of his life.

"It only takes five minutes to have a stroke, but it takes five years to recover," he once observed.

Advancing age, too, began to take its toll. There was a diagnosis of diabetes and other random health problems. He needed full-time care, which he found in full measure at the Motion Picture Home. As wonderful a place as this is — with its beautiful grounds and friendly staff — many former stars would never allow themselves to be taken there to live: to them, it would be the ultimate sign of defeat. Larry did not subscribe to this in the least. He was immensely grateful that the MPCH existed and adapted well to his new environment. There were, after all, shuffleboard tournaments, art classes and costume competitions. One year he was Bette Davis in *Whatever Happened to Baby Jane?* To assume the characterization, Larry donned a little white dress, had his face powdered and his mouth smeared with dark lipstick, and then topped it all off with a long red wig and oversized bow. In his right hand was a whiskey bottle with a nipple on top. Looking at the snapshots of this prize-winning getup, I couldn't help but ask if he had felt just the least bit embarrassed by his appearance.

"Hell," Larry smiled, "I'm used to making an ass of myself."

Twice a year he and Moe continued that practice by performing silly skits in the resident-run "Ding-a-Ling" variety shows. With his silver hair combed straight down in the bowl-cut style, Moe seemed a much older version of his celluloid self. But he and Larry could still bring down the house by performing such crowd-pleasing ditties as, "She Was Bred in Old Kentucky, but She's Just a Crumb Up Here."

As one of the few well-known personalities in residence, Larry attracted a great deal of media attention and received more than his share of visitors, including celebrities from the Hollywood community. Even when a non-celebrity (this writer, for instance) showed up at the Lodge's front desk, the receptionist would say nonchalantly, "I'll tell Mr. Fine you're here."

Since I hadn't said whom I was there to see, I wondered how she knew that it happened to be Larry.

She didn't say anything; she simply pointed to the Three Stooges T-shirt I was wearing.

Larry was also the center of attention in the facility's dining room. Each evening while savoring the featured entrée (his favorite being "Tomato Surprise"), he would entertain his fellow diners by telling jokes. The one that I especially recall involved a mink that died and was met at the Pearly Gates by St. Peter.

St. Peter said, "During your lifetime you were a wonderful mink, always conducting yourself with honor, not to mention siring five hundred children. As a reward for your exemplary lifestyle, you will be given one wish — anything your heart desires."

The little mink thought it over for a few minutes and finally said, "I know something I've always wanted: a full-length Jewish lady."

Larry stayed fairly close to the Home during these years, but on occasion he ventured out into the surrounding community to make an appearance at a school. His program consisted of one or two Stooge shorts followed by a question-and-answer period. One visit to an elementary school, in particular, touched his heart. A little girl came up to him after his presentation, hugged him and said, "I love you, Larry."

"And you know," he said to me, "I think she really meant it."

"I CAN'T DIE; I HAVEN'T SEEN *THE JOLSON STORY!*"
— Larry in *Squareheads of the Round Table* (1947)

On December 26, 1974, Larry suffered a second major stroke, and lapsed into a coma. I had heard that patients in vegetative states are often fully aware of their surroundings and benefit greatly from verbal stimulation. I therefore made a pledge to myself that I would write a letter of encouragement every day until he was well again. Recovery would be an uphill battle, I realized, but I also knew how determined Larry could be. His personal motto was "Never Give Up."

For the next three weeks I pestered the staff in the hospital's J-Ward for updates. On some days the doctors were hopeful, detecting signs of movement from the patient; on other days, he was unresponsive.

By this point, I had ceased to think of Larry simply as a famous comedian and regarded him more as a friend. In my letters I elaborated on the mundane aspects of this high school student's day-to-day activities. I remember telling him that I was taking a Driver's Education course, which I was failing. I then quoted a section of his autobiography wherein he described his determination to rally after his initial stroke. He was inspiring me, even as I sought to encourage him.

But just as there are times to fight, there also comes the inevitable time for surrender. For Larry Fine, that time came just before dawn on January 24, 1975. Nurse Marianne told me that she had finished reading the last of my letters to him only moments before he passed away.

Larry in his room at the Motion Picture Home, Woodland Hills, California, 1974. COURTESY OF SCOTT H. REBOUL

By that evening, it was all over the television news: Original Stooge Larry Fine Dies at 72.

A funeral was to be held at Forest Lawn Cemetery in Glendale on Monday, January 27th. So what if it was a school day, I told myself, I was *going*. The trouble was, I still hadn't acquired my driver's license, and no one I knew was available to take me from my home in San Diego County to Los Angeles. Early on the morning of the service I boarded a Greyhound bus, wearing one of my father's ties and carrying a sack lunch. By ten a.m. I was dropped off at the wrought-iron gates at the entrance to Forest Lawn.

It was a cold, drizzly day. A sizeable crowd made up of admirers both young and old had gathered at the cemetery's Church of the Recessional. We listened to a rabbi as he delivered the eulogy, one that failed to capture the essence of the man I knew. Afterward, the congregation was invited to file past the open casket. Seeing Larry with his eyes closed reminded me of the time he had dozed off during one of our conversations. A smaller group limited to family members and close friends later gathered in a vestibule of the Freedom Mausoleum for the interment. Larry would be in good company. In the mausoleum are some of Hollywood's biggest names: Francis X. Bushman, Chico and Gummo Marx, Clara Bow, Gracie Allen, Jeanette MacDonald and Alan Ladd.

Actual Stooges, though, were in short supply. Moe was not present: Bidding farewell to his partner was simply too emotional a prospect to consider. He was also ill with lung cancer at the time and would himself be gone within four months, at the age of seventy-eight. Joe Besser was not there either, not that I expected him to be. (He would live another thirteen years before dying of heart failure at eighty.) I did see Joe DeRita, however. He was seated Buddha-like on a marble bench, smoking a cigar and holding court with a group of reporters. (Curly-Joe would survive another eighteen years before suffering a fatal stroke just prior to his eighty-fourth birthday. Coincidentally, he passed away in the same ward of the Motion Picture Country Hospital as Larry.)

In addition to DeRita, a few former co-stars showed up to pay their last respects. Christine McIntire (a decorative singing ingénue in the 1945 Curly outing, *Micro-Phonies*) was reportedly in attendance, but I didn't recognize her. I chatted for a moment with Babe London, the comedienne who played Shemp's homely fiancée in Larry's all-time favorite short, *Scrambled Brains* (1951). Emil Sitka was there as well. (Fans will remember this versatile character actor as the minister who repeatedly warbles, "Hold hands, you lovebirds," in the 1947 gem, *Brideless Groom*.) I approached Mr. Sitka and never in my life have I met an actor who was so thrilled to be recognized. He told me that he was "in the Camarillo phone book" and to call him *anytime*. As he exited the mausoleum, I heard him exclaim to his wife, "Did you see how that kid knew who I was?"

And finally, there was Jules White, the man who had produced and directed the majority of the Stooges' shorts. Mr. White was a true motion picture pioneer, having started in the silent era with a bit part in D.W. Griffith's 1915 epic, *The Birth of a Nation*. He later guided Buster Keaton, Harry Langdon and Andy Clyde through some of their talkie efforts. In recent years he had provided the foreword to Larry's autobiography and was one of the few Columbia veterans to visit his ailing colleague. I remember calling Larry during one such visit, and hearing the excitement in his voice as he said: "Jules White is in my room *right now!*"

I felt it only appropriate that I offer this downcast gentleman my condolences for his loss.

"Excuse me, sir," I said respectfully, "but aren't you Jules White?"

His response was incredibly terse: "Yeah, I'm Jules White. What about it?"

"Uh, nothing," I said, feeling myself blush. "I'm sorry I disturbed you."

He must have realized that I was not just an autograph seeker since a short time later he walked over to me, a different person.

"We've lost quite a friend, haven't we?" he said softly.

That we had.

LON DAVIS WAS STILL IN HIS TEENS WHEN HE WAS WORKING AS A PROFESSIONAL COMIC-IMPRESSIONIST IN THE SAN DIEGO AREA. DISSATISFIED WITH THE COMEDY CLUB SCENE, LON BEGAN DEVOTING HIS TIME TO FILM RESEARCH AND ANIMAL WELFARE CAUSES; IN 1992 HE AND HIS WIFE DEBRA CO-FOUNDED A HUMANE SOCIETY. SINCE 2001 LON HAS HOSTED A WELL-RECEIVED SILENT FILM SERIES IN HIS ADOPTED CITY OF EUGENE, OREGON. HE IS THE AUTHOR OF *SILENT LIVES: 100 BIOGRAPHIES OF THE SILENT FILM ERA* (BEARMANOR MEDIA, 2008). LON AND DEBRA ARE THE CO-EDITORS OF *STOOGES AMONG US*.

A View from the Front Row

by Diana Serra Cary

I was seated in the dining room of the Motion Picture Country House with my mother. She had worked as an extra in hundreds of films and therefore qualified to become a resident of that retired actors' haven in Woodland Hills, California. It was 1971. Although she was a newcomer at the Home, Mother always seemed to be bumping into someone she had met or worked with during her Hollywood years. That particular afternoon we were seated with the Oscar-nominated director Mitchell Leisen, former RKO producer Gene Towne and a little gentleman who had recently had a major stroke. He was having trouble eating, and the food kept escaping from his mouth. The poor man: He was so embarrassed.

"You remember Larry Fine, don't you?" Mother asked.

I did not. But after a childhood spent in the spotlight I learned to acknowledge everyone I met as a familiar acquaintance.

"Nice to see you again, Larry," I said politely.

"I sure remember *you*," he said with a crooked smile, "Baby Peggy."

That was how I was billed during the 1920s when I was a child star in silent films. By the time of this meeting I was known by my current name, Diana.

"Oh, Larry," Mother gushed, "Diana has *always* wanted an autographed picture of you."

Clearly, this was not the case, but he was happy to oblige. "I'll sign it when I get back to my room," Larry said as he was being wheeled away by a nurse.

"Mother," I said under my breath, "how do I know him? Was he in pictures?"

"Of *course*!" she said. "He was one of the Three Stooges."

Malice in the Palace

My mind flashed back to 1928. I was in Chicago, headlining in vaudeville in a comedy sketch. Despite my star billing, it was a grueling existence. Repeating the same lines three and four times a day for two years, I was having almost daily mental blackouts onstage. I would emerge from these right on cue, but aware that I had not been wholly on that stage for a frighteningly long time.

A lobby still of "Baby Peggy" in vaudeville, circa 1928.
Courtesy of the Diana Serra Cary Collection

To escape the monotony of sitting around hearing the other acts over and over, my mother, sister and I would leave the theater and kill time in another one. Perhaps we'd go see a movie (King Vidor's *The Big Parade* comes to mind) or catch an opposing vaudeville bill. I saw some great comedians that way. I remember Jack Benny with his violin and Fred Allen with his wisecracks. Fred and his wife Portland, in fact, lived in the same apartment building as my mother and I in 1929.

Another comic who was a good friend of ours was Ted Healy. Healy was a monologist, and a rough one. He would stand on the stage wearing a rumpled suit and a battered fedora with the front brim turned up — that was his trademark.

As he was telling his one-liners there was a commotion coming from one of the upper boxes. Three clownish men took turns yelling out insults to Healy — right in the middle of his act! I didn't realize it at the time, but these were his stooges — Moe, Larry and Shemp. They went on in this rambunctious manner throughout Healy's turn. Some of the audience liked it; some did not. I was among the latter. This is rude, I remember thinking. How can they get away with it? I later learned that this was a carefully rehearsed comedy act, but that didn't make me like it any better.

And as I said, I wasn't alone.

Vaudeville impresarios were aspiring to attract an upper-class clientele, those individuals who frequented the "legitimate theater." The better vaudeville palaces of the time were as ornate as any castle in Spain. Architects specialized in designing and building resplendent replicas of everything from a Pharaoh's tomb to Versailles. Carpets were deep, draperies rich, pillars and stairways made of pure varicolored marbled, ceilings coffered or, simulating a night sky, studded with glittering stars. The artists who performed in these showplaces were expected to behave accordingly. There were signs posted backstage at every one of the Keith-Albee theaters that read:

NO SWEARING
NO SPITTING

I remember hearing grumblings backstage about "low" acts like Healy and his Stooges. "But," the vaudevillians would say grudgingly, "they sure do 'go over.'"

Despite his coarse onstage image, Ted Healy was a very nice man. He stayed in touch with us, even after I outgrew my vaudeville sketch. My family was living on "my" 1500-acre ranch in Wyoming in the early thirties, and Ted was on his way to Hollywood. (He later made quite a few films for MGM.) Ted and his wife Betty didn't call ahead; they just dropped by for a couple of hours. My parents didn't have a casual drink to offer as hard liquor fueled "parties" in those days of Prohibition. That must have been hard on Ted since he had the reputation of being a big drinker. When he was sober, though, he was a thoroughly pleasant individual. He politely accepted Mother's invitation to stay for lunch, and she cooked up one of her typical feasts.

HIGHER THAN A KITE

Healy's Stooges, as everyone knows, went solo and had a great career in pictures. Mother "worked extra" on a yacht in one of their early features — *The Captain Hates the Sea*, shot in July and August of 1934. This was the last film to feature John Gilbert, the once-great matinee idol whose career at Metro-Goldwyn-Mayer had been destroyed by Louis B. Mayer. The director Lewis Milestone was hoping to revive his friend's career by giving him the leading role in this film. It also gave Milestone's boss, Harry Cohn, the chance to needle his rival, Mayer. The only wild card was the troubled star's heavy drinking.

As I wrote in my autobiography: "After staying sober for the first week, the insecure Gilbert hit the bottle. Confident he could control the actor's access to liquor at sea, Milestone took the company on location, aboard a rented yacht cruising the Los Angeles harbor and Catalina Island. But his cast boasted a pride of inveterate drinkers, including the Three Stooges, who found ingenious ways to keep Gilbert's party going. The sun refused to shine, the wind blew, and the frantic director found most of his all-star cast too drunk to deliver intelligible dialogue. Six weeks later, the production costs spiraling, Cohn cabled Milestone at sea: 'HURRY UP. THE COST IS STAGGERING.'

"Milestone cabled back: 'SO IS THE CAST.'"

The all-star cast of *The Captain Hates the Sea* (1934) are (left to right): Larry Fine, Curley Howard, Moe Howard, Allison Skipworth, John Nerling, G. Pat Collins, Arthur Treacher, Leon Errol, John Gilbert, Lewis Milestone (director), Walter Connelly, Wallace Smith, Victor McLaglen, Wynne Gibson, Akim Tamiroff, Emily Fitzroy, Walter Catlett, Donald Meek and Claude Gillingwater. COURTESY OF THE DIANA SERRA CARY COLLECTION

I never really saw the shorts that the Stooges made for Columbia — not if I could help it. Certainly I respected their skills as physical comics, but I preferred biographical pictures, the kind that starred such actors as Paul Muni and Leslie Howard.

Not surprisingly, my son Mark (born in 1961) loved the Three Stooges on television. So I gave *him* the signed picture of Larry. He still has it, I believe.

DIANA SERRA CARY (THE FORMER "BABY PEGGY") WAS ONE OF THE TWO MAJOR CHILD STARS DURING THE SILENT ERA, THE OTHER BEING JACKIE COOGAN. LONG RETIRED FROM PERFORMING, MRS. CARY HAS EARNED A SOLID REPUTATION AS A HISTORIAN. SHE HAS LECTURED EXTENSIVELY ON THE SILENT FILM INDUSTRY AND IS A REGULAR AT INTERNATIONAL CINEMA CONVENTIONS. HER AUTOBIOGRAPHY, *WHAT EVER HAPPENED TO BABY PEGGY?*, WHICH WAS ORIGINALLY PUBLISHED BY ST. MARTIN'S PRESS IN 1996, IS BEING REISSUED BY BEARMANOR MEDIA IN 2008.

MY PAL MOE

BY BOB BERNET

Like most twelve-year-old boys, I had been a big fan of The Three
Stooges since I first saw them poking, gouging and slapping
each other around like live-action cartoons. Late one evening in
May of 1968, my mother awakened me to tell me that my heroes
were on television. They were guests on *The Joey Bishop Show*, a
late-night talk show on ABC that ran opposite the *Tonight Show*
with Johnny Carson.

A little groggy, I staggered to the television surprised to see the
familiar trio throwing pies and creating mayhem — *and* in color. I
noticed that they had aged a little since the old black and white
days, but I was glad to know that they were still performing. It was
a pleasant surprise to know they were still going strong. I was now
anxious to know when I could see them on television again. One
way to find out, I figured, was to write them and ask. Soon after
sending a letter simply addressed to *The Three Stooges, Hollywood,
California*, I received an answer in the mail. It was a handwritten
letter from the head Stooge himself, Moe Howard.

Dear Friend Bobby,
Thank you for your letter.
We expect to be on the Joey Bishop Show *on June 26 or close to*
that date.
Watch for the date in TV Guide.

All the best,
Sincerely,
Moe

Thousands of fans received this promotional photo of the latter-day Stooges. The signatures, incidentally, do not match those of Moe, Larry and Curly-Joe. COURTESY OF THE SCOTT H. REBOUL COLLECTION.

I could hardly believe that I had received a personal letter from one of my favorite film stars! I proudly showed it to my summer baseball buddies and friends from school. But when I did, many of them tried to tell me that someone as important and busy as Moe did not have time to answer fan letters. Instead, they insisted, the letter must have been written by someone who worked for him. I refused to believe that and continued to write.

I figured if Moe answered the first letter, he just might answer a second. Twenty-five letters later during the summer of 1973, I had the special opportunity of finally meeting my famous pen pal. After graduating from high school in May of that year, a friend of mine by the name of Bill Janin and I decided to take a road trip to California that summer. Hoping for an outside chance to meet Moe, I wrote and told him of my plans. I soon received a reply that included a telephone number suggesting that I call when I arrived in Los Angeles. If he were in town, Moe said in his letter, he would be glad to arrange a meeting. Needless to say, I was soon on my way to California.

California, Here We Come

The journey unraveled into a series of events that I would never have imagined possible. We made arrangements to stay with relatives between Dallas and Los Angeles. After some side trips to Albuquerque, the Grand Canyon and Las Vegas, we finally arrived in Los Angeles. We stayed with some friends of my family who lived in the Brentwood area just off Sunset Boulevard. It was a beautiful part of the city and not far, I was to soon learn, from Moe's house.

Not long after arriving, I decided to call the telephone number that Moe had given me. The number belonged to Joan Maurer, Moe's daughter, who was helping to manage Moe's busy schedule.

Fortunately, she was home when I called. It was a thrilling moment when she answered. Trying to remain calm and intelligible, I explained who I was and why I was calling. I was not prepared for her reply: "Oh, yes," she said with a pause. "I believe Dad has mentioned you before — the young man from Texas."

So, Moe really *did* know who I was! At that moment, I felt as if all those letters had suddenly come to life. I was getting close to meeting the person I had been writing to for the past five years. Joan asked how long I planned to be in town.

"Until I get to meet your Dad," is what I wanted to say, but I restrained myself and told her that I planned to be in town for about ten days.

"Dad's not here at the moment, but should be in town during your visit." I was thrilled. "Why don't you give me the telephone number where you are staying," she suggested, "and I will call you back when I know more about his schedule."

I was all too anxious to accommodate. After exchanging good-byes, all kinds of thoughts entered my mind. Would I really be able to meet Moe? If so, would I meet him at an office? A studio? A restaurant? What would he look like? Would he be the same Moe I had grown up watching on television and in the movies? I decided not to fret over those concerns. I was seventeen years old and in Los Angeles to have a great time no matter what happened. Somehow, I knew that things would work out.

LOS ANGELES

A couple of days passed while my friend Bill and I stayed busy exploring Los Angeles for the first time. The beach was one of the first places on the list to visit, so we drove west on Sunset Boulevard until we found it. The Pacific Ocean was unexpectedly cooler than the warm waters of the Gulf of Mexico that I was familiar with in Texas. About all I remember was a crowded beach scattered with beautiful people and a shark warning that scattered them even further.

We also spent some time driving up and down Hollywood Boulevard and Sunset Boulevard between Beverly Hills and the Hollywood Freeway, gawking at all the sights that were so familiar from the movies and television. Sunset Boulevard was lined with billboards advertising movies. I had never seen films advertised that way before. This was 1973. Such sophisticated marketing techniques had not made their way to Texas yet.

On our way home from comparing our hand prints and shoe sizes in the cement at Graumann's Chinese Theater one night, an exotic maroon and chrome-laden automobile rolled up to the right of us at a red light on Sunset Boulevard. I did not recognize this make of car. After driving alongside this unusual car for a couple of miles, I noticed that the license plate read, "DRUNKY." I was in the passenger seat and was curious to steal an unsuspecting glance at this flamboyant driver. At the next opportunity, I looked to my right and suddenly found myself eye-to-eye with Dean Martin!

"That's Dean Martin!" I blurted out.

"You're kidding!" said Bill as we maneuvered through the winding curves on Sunset Boulevard.

We kept even with Martin for the next few blocks long enough to become pests. We surmised that the person sitting next to him was his new young wife. When he realized that we had recognized him, he quickly sped away.

Coincidentally, we saw the car parked in front of the Bel Air Country Club the very next day. The valet allowed me to snap a photo of it. We later learned that it was a custom-built Stutz Blackhawk. There were very few made.

The Telephone Rings

Three or four days had passed since my telephone conversation with Joan Maurer. We had all just sat down for breakfast when the telephone rang. The lady of the house left the table to answer the phone in an adjacent room.

"Hello," I heard her say. "Yes, he's here; just a moment." I assumed the telephone call was for her husband, but she was looking at *me*.

"Bobby," she called out as she waved me to the phone. "I think it's Moe."

There was no time to panic. She handed me the receiver.

"Hello," I said.

"Bobby?" I heard the familiar voice say on the other end of the line. "This is Moe. How are you?"

It had finally happened. I was actually talking to the head Stooge himself, Moe Howard! The man I had only imagined getting the chance to meet. It was all coming true.

The telephone conversation was short. We made arrangements to meet on the following Saturday at one o'clock at his house. Moe spent the remainder of the conversation giving me directions. He also gave me his telephone number in case we got lost. I now had directions to Moe's house. It was only Thursday and we were not scheduled to meet for another two days. Bill and I decided to drive to Moe's house that day so that we would be sure to find it on Saturday. It turned out to be a good idea because it took several twists and turns to get there. We also discovered that we were staying just fifteen minutes away from Moe. It would be two more days before we would make that memorable trip.

Insights into Comedy

It was Saturday afternoon about one o'clock when we arrived at 9061 Thrasher Avenue in the Hollywood Hills. Moe's neighborhood was located high above the old Sunset Strip off of Doheny Drive. His street was on a hill that overlooked the city — the kind of view that is popular in movies that present Los Angeles from a Lover's

Moe Howard, circa 1973. COURTESY OF JOAN HOWARD MAUER.

Lane-type vantage point with rows upon rows of lights shining in the night.

We parked the car in the driveway which led to a car port that housed a big Cadillac DeVille and a little Mazda RX3. We discovered later that the Mazda was Moe's car.

After ringing the bell, the door opened and a tiny woman greeted us and ushered us into the front hallway. This was Moe's wife, Helen.

Far down the hallway, I could see a little man walking toward us with silver hair combed down in a bowl haircut.

"Which one is Bobby?" he asked.

After five years and stacks of letters, I was finally meeting Moe Howard!

Helen was closing the door behind us when it suddenly occurred to me that Moe had no idea what I looked like. My scrapbooks were filled with *his* pictures, but I had never thought to send him *mine*.

"I'm Bobby," I announced while reaching to shake his hand.

Just over five feet tall, Moe appeared to be sizing up my six-foot frame. "Who put you way the hell up there?" he asked.

Not far from the front door was a single volume of the *World Book* Encyclopedia. It carefully rested across a bookstand not unlike a Bible and was opened to the section on Comedy. *World Book* had used a photo of the Three Stooges in their recent editions to illustrate the definition of comedy. Moe chuckled when I glanced at the book. "If the Encyclopedia recognizes the Stooges as the definition of comedy," he said, "then who am I to argue?" With that, Moe directed us into his living room.

I soon felt that I was in the company of an old friend. He gave us a tour of their home including his study which was full of Three Stooges memorabilia from their two-hundred plus films. I noticed a large portrait on the wall of his study. It was a beautiful oil of Moe in character. He said that it had been painted by a teenage girl who had surprised him with it as a gift. He seemed to be truly appreciative of the attention and goodwill that the fans displayed.

The walls of Moe's study seemed covered with hundreds of pictures from films and personal appearances. I was looking at one particular montage of stills from their shorts that included pictures of Shemp. Moe said that Shemp was a gifted actor who really could not be compared to Curly. He also pointed out that Shemp had been quite successful on his own before re-joining the Stooges after Curly became ill.

By chance, I had seen Shemp in other roles without the Stooges, but had never known much about him otherwise. Now I was getting first-hand information. Moe did not offer much information on Larry other than to report that he was at the Motion Picture Country Home in nearby Woodland Hills and responding well to therapy for the stroke that he suffered in 1970.

Ted Healy and his Stooges in a scene from *Beer and Pretzels* (Metro-Goldwyn-Mayer, 1933). COURTESY OF THE COLE JOHNSON SLAPSTICK ARCHIVE.

We eventually settled in the living room. Moe sat on the hearth while Bill and I sat on a sofa to Moe's right. Helen was very gracious and prepared some finger sandwiches and soft drinks for us. The house was all on one level, but was very spacious. I remember there were lots of windows and the sunshine poured in. Interestingly, the Watergate congressional hearings were in full swing at the time and they were on the television in his living room at the moment.

"Isn't this something?" he said pointing to the hearings. Not knowing what side of the political fence Moe was on, I was reluctant to say anything about Watergate for fear of saying the wrong thing. I just mumbled something that indicated that I was as taken aback by all these political shenanigans as he was.

Being the Stooge fans that we were, it was not long before we started bombarding him with all of the familiar questions that he had certainly heard thousands of times. But the answers were new to me. In 1973, there was relatively little information written about the Three Stooges and their history. Moe's autobiography,

Moe Howard and the 3 Stooges, would not be published until 1977, two years after his death. If it had not been for his daughter, Joan, the book would not have been published at all. The only information I had about the Stooges was from Moe's letters and standard studio biographies that he would send with his letters when my questions became too general such as, "How did you get started in show business?" I must have tried his patience at times with all those questions and letters.

We asked one question after another and listened to him as he sat on the hearth sharing stories about his brothers, Curly and Shemp. He said that Curly was a "bad study," which meant that he had trouble memorizing his lines. As a result, he would often improvise when he forgot a line and might drop to the floor and spin around like a top or bark or make some spontaneous noise. We have all seen him do it, but now we know how it originated.

Moe also revealed that Lou Costello used to "borrow" Three Stooges films from Columbia Pictures from time to time, presumably to study Curly. Inevitably, similar characteristics would appear in Abbott and Costello films.

Moe had nothing but kind words to say about his brothers. He described Curly as very kind, gentle and happy-go-lucky. He also said that he was a true comic.

"Many people don't know that there is a difference between a comic and a comedian," Moe told us. "A comedian is someone like Bob Hope or Johnny Carson — people who are very gifted at delivering jokes or lines that are written for them. A comic is someone who is naturally funny — someone who can make *any* situation funny. Curly was a comic."

I had never heard that distinction before and I will never forget it.

We asked Moe if the Stooges followed a script in their Columbia shorts since their antics often appeared so spontaneous and impromptu. He said that yes, all the Stooges comedies were carefully scripted. A script usually originated with the Stooges presenting a treatment or detailed story idea to the writers. The writers would then put together a twenty-nine page draft of a script. The Stooges would go over the draft and make the necessary changes and re-submit it to the writers. The writers would then return with the final draft. A typical short took about three days to shoot, but the

Although they may have seemed "off the cuff," the Stooges' two-reelers were in fact carefully scripted. This is a sample first page from one such script, *Cookoo Cavaliers* (Columbia Pictures, 1940), written by Ewart Adamson. COURTESY OF BOB BERNET

PRODUCTION #4006

FADE IN:

1   MED. LONG SHOT:

Of small truck.

DISSOLVE TO:

2   MED. CLOSE SHOT - TRUCK:

With sign painted on the side:

"FRESH FISH"

Over sign we hear the sound of a FISH HORN, very sour, and a voice calling: "FRESH FISH!" The truck continues slowly down the street.

3   CLOSE SHOT - THREE STOOGES ON FRONT SEAT OF TRUCK:

Moe is driving, Curly is blowing the fish horn, and Larry is calling: "FRESH FISH". Each time Curly blows the horn, he turns toward Moe and blasts him in the ear. Moe reacts to this once or twice, then grabs the horn from Curly and belts him over the head with it, bending the horn out of shape. As Curly looks at the horn, we hear a woman's voice yelling o.s.

WOMAN'S VOICE
Yoo hoo -- fishman!

The boys look around and Moe brings the truck to a stop.

4   MED. LONG SHOT:

As the Stooges scramble off their truck and run around to the back end, a woman enters scene at the back of the truck.

5   MED. GROUP SHOT:

As the Stooges run into the woman at the rear of the truck.

WOMAN
What kind of fish have you?

CURLY
Tuna fish - smelt fish - dog fish, cat fish - - -

During this Larry has opened the back door of the truck.

A delightfully candid shot of the Howard Brothers. COURTESY OF BOB BERNET

entire process usually took three or four weeks. Moe was quick to point out that although the Stooges were definitely scripted, they rarely rehearsed in order not to lose the spontaneity of the moment.

At one point in the conversation, we began talking about the films that placed the Stooges in high society situations. They always resulted in the upper class being brought down to the Stooges' level, and often resulted in a massive pie fight.

"Our formula," Moe said, "was to pull the rug from beneath dignity without hurting anyone. We wanted to show that the rich guy was basically no different than the little guy."

You Ought to Be in Pictures

After visiting for a little over an hour, I asked Moe if we could take a few pictures.

"It wouldn't be the first time," he said, leading us out into the sunshine.

I brought along a small Super 8mm movie camera and a small Kodak still camera to chronicle the event. Moe was very accommodating and immediately began "directing" by telling us where to stand and when to start shooting.

He was a real sport as he clowned around in front of the camera, making faces and poking his fingers into the lens. I think Moe had as much fun as we did.

While we were outside taking pictures, I asked him if he was often recognized in public. He then shared a quick story about a little boy who had recently recognized him in traffic while at a stoplight. Pointing out the car window, the little boy cried out, "Mommy! Mommy! There's Moe!" Moe gestured back to the little boy with the classic two-finger poke in-the-eyes routine.

I regret not snapping more photos and shooting more footage. The home movie is just over one minute. All in all, the pictures turned out well, but the memories are even better.

SAYING GOODBYE

On May 4, 1975 Moe Howard died of lung cancer. I was deeply saddened when I heard the news on television. Reflecting on my long-distance friendship with Moe, he did not appear to be the type of person who would open his heart or his home to fans. But the more I have learned about him over the years, the more I have come to realize that the man I met was the true Moe Howard. He may have come across as gruff and "all business," but underneath, he was a giving and caring man who truly enjoyed entertaining others.

The following morning I left Dallas to attend Moe's funeral service at Hillside Memorial Park in Los Angeles. It was an impulsive decision, but I have never regretted it. I wanted to be there to say good-bye.

I arrived at the sanctuary so early that no one else was there. After thirty interminable minutes, a man appeared in what looked like a janitor's uniform. I'm glad he came when he did. He provided some light-hearted moments to an otherwise somber occasion. With a thick Australian accent, he introduced himself as one of the groundskeepers. He noted that the "Howard service" would not commence for another two hours and offered to give me a tour of the cemetery and introduce me to some of the famous inhabitants.

As we zipped around the grounds in a golf cart, my guide pointed to some of the ornate monuments marking the graves. A particularly garish one had been designed by the great entertainer Al Jolson — for himself. The structure is so large, in fact, that it can easily be seen from the adjacent San Diego Freeway. The monument also includes a bronze statue of Jolson on one knee singing his signature song, "Swanee."

Our next stop was inside a mausoleum. At the far end of one of the main hallways was a black marble tomb that my guide referred to as a "sarcophagus." I noticed that there was no name on the tomb. This was the final resting place for Jack Benny. Mr. Benny had passed away six months before at the age of eighty. For decades, however, the comedian had insisted that he was only thirty-nine.

"And you know what?" the groundskeeper said with surprise; "he *looked* thirty-nine!"

On the way back to the chapel, I was whisked by the graves of Harpo Marx, Jeff Chandler and others. I was soon back at the chapel where people had begun to gather for Moe's service. I thanked my host for the tour, signed the attendance register and took a seat in the sanctuary. By the time the service began, there were no seats available. People had to stand in the back of the building.

It was a beautiful afternoon. The sun was shining through the floor-to-ceiling windows of the sanctuary just like it streamed into Moe's home on the day of our visit almost two years before.

With his casket in the middle of the altar, Moe was eulogized by friends who recounted fond memories of a full life. They talked about the charitable organizations that Moe had worked with; his unlimited energy and zest for life and how he had worked tirelessly to complete his book only days before his death. On a solemn note, they also said how much he was going to be missed.

After the service, people quietly gathered in the afternoon sun and visited with one another. I noticed Joe DeRita smoking a cigar and chatting with fellow entertainer Mousie Garner, who was once considered as the replacement for Shemp. Moe's casket was soon brought out for interment in the nearby outdoor mausoleum. It appeared as though members of Moe's family were his pallbearers, including his two young grandsons. When the casket was brought out of the chapel by the pallbearers, Mrs. Howard was visibly and understandably upset. It was a touching moment.

As family and friends gathered around the interment site, I noticed an elderly man with a full head of white hair standing with the family. He struck a strong resemblance to Shemp — that is, if Shemp had lived to be an old man. I later learned it was Jack Howard, the last of the Howard brothers.

The outdoor service was rather brief. A prayer was offered by the rabbi and Moe was laid to rest in the Garden of Memories. Less than six months later, Helen Howard passed away on October 31, 1975.

REFLECTING ON MOE

As the years have passed and I look back on that period in my life and realize how fortunate I was to have met Moe. I doubt that anyone in show business today would take the time that he did to cultivate a friendship with a fan. He taught me a great lesson in humility. Moe did not place himself above the crowd. He managed to remain one of us. Here was a very successful individual who was under no obligation to spend time with me or any other fan. But he did. He responded to my letters, sent stacks of pictures and invited me into his home. For that, he was quite special.

He was simply . . . My Pal, Moe.

Bob Bernet (center) is reunited with Moe Howard's son Paul and daughter Joan at the Stoogeum in Spring House, Pennsylvania, in April 2006.
COURTESY OF BOB BERNET

BOB BERNET IS AN EDUCATIONAL TELEVISION PRODUCER IN DALLAS, TEXAS. HIS PROGRAMS COVER SUCH TOPICS AS HEALTHCARE, FIRE AND EMERGENCY PROCEDURES AND LAW ENFORCEMENT INSTRUCTION. BOB IS A MULTI-FACETED PRODUCER. HE OVERSEES THE SCRIPTS, BUDGETS, CREWS, LOCATIONS, GRAPHICS, AND SUPERVISES THE TAPING AND EDITING. ON OCCASION HE SERVES AS THE ON-CAMERA HOST OF HIS PROGRAMS AND FREQUENTLY PROVIDES VOICE-OVER NARRATION.

THE STOOGES: LIVE AND IN PERSON!

BY STEVE STOLIAR

I spent my early childhood in St. Louis, where celebrity sightings were in short supply during the 1950s and early '60s, so it was no trivial matter when, in the summer of 1962, it was announced that The Three Stooges would be making a personal appearance in my hometown as part of a promotional tour for their latest theatrical endeavor, *The Three Stooges In Orbit*. This was a colossal thrill for me, because I'd recently become a major Stooges fan after seeing their short films on TV. But when I saw them in person, outdoors, under the glare of the afternoon sun, there were certain "discrepancies" that puzzled me.

For one thing, they looked so much *older* in person than they did on our black-and-white Zenith. For another, Curly-Joe didn't look much like the Curly I was familiar with. He had the requisite rotund figure, but the *face* was all wrong, somehow. At one point, Moe made a joke about how Larry combed his hair with an egg-beater. It was a funny line, but it didn't really *work* because the Larry I was staring at had only a few strands of gray hair, slicked back along the sides of his head — hardly the unruly bird's nest I was used to seeing on TV.

Of course, what I didn't realize at the time was that the shorts I'd been laughing at were — even then — twenty or thirty years old, and that the original Curly had ceased acting in 1947 after suffering a stroke. Moe urged us to ask our parents to take us to see their latest picture, and made a *big* point of admonishing us not to try poking each other in the eyes at home — that they were professionals and they had a special secret way of doing it so that it didn't really hurt. It was a brief, but magical, moment for me.

In 1962 Curly-Joe, Larry and Moe embarked on a hectic east-coast tour with the RKO Theatre chain to promote their latest feature, *The Three Stooges Meet Hercules*. COURTESY OF GARY LASSIN

I later found out that the Stooge/St. Louis connection had a much more personal relevance: I was distantly related to St. Louis-born Joe Besser, who was an official Stooge in the mid-50s, after Shemp died! Alas, the connection was only through marriage, on my paternal grandmother's side of the family, and I never did meet him, although I heard he was a sweet man.

A FINAL APPEARANCE

Ten years after the St. Louis incident, after our family had moved to California, Moe and Larry made a personal appearance at my school, Taft High in Woodland Hills. Like the original Curly, Larry had recently suffered a stroke and was confined to a wheelchair. Moe was still quite spry, although he looked every inch his seventy-five years.

To start things off, *Micro-Phonies* was screened because, as Moe explained, it was their favorite short. Then Larry was wheeled out, to thunderous applause, and the two of them began — or tried to begin — an old routine:

MOE: "Well look who's here!"

LARRY: "They call me Tex!"

MOE: "Why do they call you Tex? You're not from Texas!"

(Long pause, while Larry looks puzzled and uncomfortable.)

MOE: "I say you're not from Texas. Why would they call you Tex?"

(Another long pause, as the discomfort spreads throughout the audience. Finally, with Larry obviously unable to come up with the punchline, Moe tries to save the bit.)

MOE: "Is it because, since you're from Louisiana, they'd have to call you Louise?"

LARRY: (sheepishly) ". . . yeah . . ."

Despite the touch-and-go delivery, the audience reacted enthusiastically, giving two of The Three Stooges the support and adulation they so richly deserved. They even stayed to sign a few autographs.

Not surprisingly, Larry's health continued to deteriorate and he slipped away three years after that appearance. More surprisingly, Moe died only a few months after Larry, of lung cancer. By then, I'd been working for the founding member of another illustrious comedy team — Groucho Marx — as his personal secretary and archivist, for over a year, rubbing shoulders with the likes of Zeppo, Gummo, George Burns, Mae West, and Bob Hope. As with the Stooges, seeing Groucho and his extant brothers in decline reminded me of how jarring that chasm between perception and reality can be. But I'll always cherish the thrill I got in 1962 when The Three Stooges came to my hometown.

STEVE STOLIAR IS A WRITER/PRODUCER IN LOS ANGELES. HE SPENT HIS COLLEGE YEARS AS GROUCHO MARX'S PERSONAL SECRETARY AND ARCHIVIST. HIS MEMORIES OF THAT SINGULAR EXPERIENCE CAN BE FOUND IN HIS 1996 BOOK, *RAISED EYEBROWS: MY YEARS INSIDE GROUCHO'S HOUSE*. IN ADDITION TO HAVING WRITTEN FOR NUMEROUS TELEVISION SERIES INCLUDING *MURDER, SHE WROTE* AND *SIMON & SIMON*, STEVE PRODUCED THE DOCUMENTARY *KING: MAN OF PEACE IN A TIME OF WAR* AND THE TWO-DISC DVD SET, *SHEMP COCKTAIL: A TOAST TO THE ORIGINAL STOOGE* (PASSPORT VIDEO, 2008).

A Rose by Any Other Name

by Rose Marie

My last name was originally Mazzetta. But my father said, "We can't use that," so he changed it to Curley. He had an uncle who was a fight promoter and he thought that would be a good professional name — certainly better than Mazzetta. Consequently, I became known as Rose Marie Curley.

I was in vaudeville then, and I was touring on the RKO Circuit. So were the original Three Stooges: Moe Howard, Larry Fine and Jerry Howard (This was just after their split with Ted Healy). We were on the road eight or ten weeks together, and during that time, we became good friends. Jerry was always teasing me. And my father and the Stooges were always pulling gags on one another. One time — I swear this is true — my father nailed their shoes to the floor! They got their entrance cue and they couldn't get on stage . . . They finally had to go on barefoot! I remember hearing Jerry say, "Hey, *Curley*, cut that out!"

Before long, everyone started calling Jerry "Curley" — after my father.

You know, I've never told that story before, not even when I wrote my autobiography.

I was discovered while I was singing on the beach in Atlantic City and put on the air by the manager of radio station WPG. As a result of that, I was signed by WMCA for *The Orbach Hour*, and *that* led to a contract with the NBC Blue Network. My billing (which was suggested by Evelyn Nesbitt Thaw) was "Baby Rose Marie, the Child Wonder." My coast-to-coast radio show could be heard every Sunday afternoon on Station WJZ at 12:15. It was a straightforward show — just a piano player, an announcer and me. My theme song,

Rose Marie Curley as she appeared in the all-star extravaganza,
International House **(Paramount, 1933).** COURTESY OF THE COLE JOHNSON
SLAPSTICK ARCHIVE

For the first fourteen Three Stooges shorts, Jerry Howard was billed as "Curley," the exact spelling of Rose Marie's last name. After typists in the secretarial pool repeatedly left out the "e," Curley was changed to "Curly." ©COLUMBIA PICTURES, 1934

I think, was "Baby Shoes." I was six years old at the time. But listeners would write in saying, "That's not a child; that's a forty-five-year-old midget. No child sings like that."

NBC was part of RKO and I was signed to NBC's artist bureau. They laid out a fifty-two-week tour. I would be appearing in all of the RKO theatres. This was NBC's way of proving that I wasn't a midget. It was on that tour that I met the Three Stooges. I enjoyed their act very much and I liked them offstage. They were the nicest guys you could ever meet.

I never really lost touch with them, not really. Moe and I did a scene for a picture that my friend Morey Amsterdam produced in 1966: *Don't Worry, We'll Think of a Title*. I think everybody in Hollywood was in that film, though.

The last time I was ever around one of the Stooges was at the Motion Picture Country Home. Larry was there, and it was good to see him again. I was visiting one day to do what I always do — sing and entertain. Afterward, Larry and I sat down and began to reminisce about our days in vaudeville. We talked for hours! I loved him. He used to treat me like I was still a young lady.

Today the Three Stooges are even more popular than they ever were. And that's well deserved.

ROSE MARIE IS BEST KNOWN FOR HER THRICE-EMMY-NOMINATED ROLE AS SALLY ROGERS ON *THE DICK VAN DYKE SHOW*. SHE ALSO APPEARED REGULARLY ON *HOLLYWOOD SQUARES*, *THE DORIS DAY SHOW* AND VARIOUS OTHER TELEVISION SERIES. MEMENTOS FROM HER SHOW BUSINESS CAREER (INCLUDING HER SIGNATURE HAIR BOWS) ARE NOW IN THE SMITHSONIAN INSTITUTION IN WASHINGTON, D.C. HER AUTOBIOGRAPHY, *HOLD THE ROSES*, WAS PUBLISHED BY THE UNIVERSITY OF KENTUCKY PRESS IN 2002.

PAPA SHEMP

BY SANDIE HOWARD

Today at any given time — whether on a television talk show or a comedy series — someone, somewhere is mentioning the Three Stooges. Everyone loves them! Their popularity only seems to grow with the passage of time. Two members of the team — Moe and Curly Howard — are my great uncles. And the original Stooge — Shemp Howard — is my grandfather.

Shemp died in 1955, so growing up, I knew him primarily from watching the Three Stooges shorts, which aired every weekday afternoon on Channel 52 in Los Angeles. My sister Jill and I could hardly believe we were related to those funny guys on TV.

"Look girls," our mother Geri would say, "There's your Papa Shemp!"

Of course, having famous relatives isn't so unusual — at least it wasn't in our neighborhood. We were surrounded by movie stars, and we were sure we shared the same feelings as their children and grandchildren. It was quite common for tour buses filled with sightseers to stop dead center in front of our house. We decided to capitalize on this by setting up a lemonade stand. The tourists would snap photos and point; they weren't interested in our ice-cold concoction, made from fresh-squeezed lemons picked from Shemp's carefully nurtured trees. We smiled back at our visitors before running into the house to tell our mom. To this day, tour buses continue to stop at Shemp's former residence. The lemonade stand, however, is no longer in business.

FAMILY MAN

Shemp had one child — our father, Mort. He didn't go into show business, although he was as multi-talented as his father, and was a genius in his own right. He was actually accepted into a prominent university when he was fourteen years old. A terrific writer, he wrote scripts for Shemp — just for the fun of it. Later he corresponded with President John F. Kennedy. Ultimately, he owned and operated gas stations, including the first "self-serve" gas station in America. Mort died suddenly of cancer in 1972. He was only forty-three.

Shemp's wife Gertrude was known as "Babe," the same nickname, incidentally, that was bestowed on Shemp's brother, Curly. Babe started out in vaudeville; she was part of a popular song-and-dance act known as "The Gertrude Frank Girls." We're not sure why, but Babe found talking about the past to be a painful experience. Nevertheless, every so often she would share a memorable story of

Shemp kisses the bride (His new daughter-in-law, Geri Mankoff) at her wedding to Mort Howard. Also pictured (left to right) are Geri's grandparents, parents and sister. Standing next to Mort is his mother (and Shemp's wife) Gertrude, who was called "Babe." Ciro's nightclub, Los Angeles, California, February 18, 1951. COURTESY OF SANDIE AND JILL HOWARD

her life with Shemp. One involved Babe volunteering as an Air Raid Warden during World War II. It was her duty to patrol the streets of their Toluca Lake neighborhood at the midnight hour. The residents were instructed to tightly shutter their homes and not let a single ray of light pierce the darkness. The Air Raid siren would sound — its deafening roar sent chills up and down the spines of anyone within earshot. When that alarm went off, Shemp would dart under the piano with lightning speed. He huddled there, shaking with fear.

"Babe, is it safe yet?" he would yell out. "Can I come out now?"

Shemp, Babe said affectionately, was just a "Big 'fraidy cat."

It's now well known that poor Shemp suffered from a host of phobias, including stage-fright. He routinely threw up before each and every performance. And his fear of riding in automobiles is legendary. He refused to get behind the wheel of a car after he crashed through a storefront window while being taught to drive by his brother, Moe. Then there was the time the Stooges had to share the same movie set with a lion! Shemp was simply petrified of that big cat. He insisted that the prop man place a thick plate of glass between him and the lion before he did his scene. The next time you see *Hold That Lion!* you'll know that the look of terror on Shemp's face was genuine.

LASTING IMPRESSIONS

For recreation, Shemp regularly went to "the fights," although it could hardly have been a relaxing experience for him. He would act out the entire bout from his ringside seat! The referee made a show of stepping out of the ring to towel Shemp off between rounds. Shemp, you see, was a born performer. He loved being "on." Everything he did was hilarious. Like the great comic he was, he knew how to use his body to get laughs — even the way he walked into a room was funny. Out of character, he was a serious, soft-spoken individual. He gave his time freely to charitable causes. And he was always respectful of his fans. He was never too busy to sign an autograph or pose for a picture.

When Shemp died, Babe became very lonely, even though our

**The Stooges and Geri Howard on the set of *Cuckoo on the Choo Choo*
(Columbia, 1952).** COURTESY OF SANDIE AND JILL HOWARD

family was quite close. She survived him by more than thirty years,
and after she passed away, we discovered a personal diary hidden
beneath her mattress. It delves into her marriage and includes
anecdotes of spending time on the road with the Stooges. It is
exquisitely written and has yet to be told. One day we hope to put
these memories into book form — along with Shemp's comprehensive
press clippings — for all to read.

SANDIE AND JILL HOWARD ARE HELPING TO PRESERVE THEIR LATE
GRANDFATHER'S COMIC LEGACY BY OPERATING A WEB SITE IN HIS HONOR
(WWW.SHEMPCOMPANY.COM). THEIR PERSONAL MEMORIES ARE INCLUDED ON THE
PASSPORT VIDEO DVD SET, *SHEMP COCKTAIL: A TOAST TO THE ORIGINAL STOOGE*.

A TALE FROM THE WEST

BY ADAM WEST

In 1965 the Three Stooges made their last theatrical feature. It was a western with an appropriate working title: "The Three Stooges Meet the Gunslingers." But between the time the film wrapped and the time it was released, somebody in marketing decided a better title would be *The Outlaws IS Coming!* It was a take-off on a promotional campaign for a film that was already two years old, Alfred Hitchcock's "*The Birds* Is Coming!" In the end, it didn't matter what it was called — it turned out to be a hit. And, as part of the cast, I got to know the Stooges and watch them in action.

What a wonderful experience it was to make that silly film. I remember showing up one morning — very early — for the first day of the shoot at the Columbia Ranch. I had on my western duds and I walked out on the street where most of the action would take place. There was Larry Fine sitting in a director's chair. His wife was yelling at him about something — I don't know what. He looked like he was pretty much used to that.

What immediately struck me about the Stooges was how different they were from their screen images. They were very serious off camera. They were really very serious artists in their own way. Moe Howard, for example, was nothing like the temperamental bully he portrayed. When I talked with him, he struck me as a kind man, and an articulate one. He was almost professorial as he discussed the Stooges' approach to comedy. Larry was a warmer individual than Moe. He seemed to have something to say to everybody on the set. Joe DeRita, who was "Curly" at that time, was the most gregarious of the three. He was extremely outgoing and communicative.

A scene from *The Outlaws Is Coming!* ©COLUMBIA PICTURES, 1965

Plenty of wacko things happened on the set of *The Outlaws IS Coming!* Playing the outlaws were hosts from Stooge television shows from around the country. Norman Maurer figured that this would help the movie's promotion if he flew them to Hollywood and put them in the film! With about twenty of these guys competing for attention, it made for a fun atmosphere. I think the funniest incident, though, happened after the last scene was shot. The main thrust of the plot was that the Stooges and I were trying to save the endangered buffalo. At the wrap party, Moe announces: "Everyone is invited to my place for a buffalo barbeque!"

Nothing better exemplifies these three Restless Knights than that remark.

I never really spent much time with Moe, Larry and Joe away from the set. People don't often do that in Hollywood. After spending eighteen hours a day with your co-stars, you pretty much just want to get away from them. But I *wanted* to go home with the Stooges every night.

They just wouldn't let me.

ADAM WEST IS BEST KNOWN FOR HIS PORTRAYAL OF THE CLASSIC BATMAN IN THE TELEVISION SERIES AND THE 1966 FEATURE. TODAY, ADAM IS IN DEMAND AS A TOP VOICE-OVER ARTIST FOR A NUMBER OF ANIMATED SERIES, SUCH AS *THE SIMPSONS, FAIRLY ODD PARENTS* AND MOST NOTABLY *FAMILY GUY*, IN WHICH HE PLAYS THE HILARIOUSLY DELUSIONAL "MAYOR ADAM WEST." FOR MORE INFORMATION ON THIS POP-CULTURE ICON, GO TO WWW.ADAMWEST.COM. THE ABOVE ACCOUNT WAS BASED ON AN INTERVIEW WITH ADAM WEST BY PRODUCER PAUL GIERUCKI. IT CAN BE SEEN IN THE 2004 DOCUMENTARY, *STOOGES: THE MEN BEHIND THE MAYHEM* (WWW.LAUGHSMITH.COM.)

THE STOOGES: A FAMILY LEGACY

BY RICK LERTZMAN

You've heard it said many times before: Men love the Three Stooges and women hate them.

There are exceptions to this rule, of course, but generally speaking, I think it's true. Take my wife (*Please!*). She is completely bewildered by their style of comedy. Just the *sound* of one of their films annoys her. I have officially been consigned to watching the Stooges in my office, with the door tightly shut. I think she's even looked into the possibility of having my television sanctuary soundproofed.

My fascination with the team goes back to my youth. I watched them on television, collected 16mm prints of their films and read every available bit of information about their lives and careers (mostly contained in Leonard Maltin's wonderful books). And I wasn't alone in my admiration. In the mid-1960s, the Three Stooges were the idols of most pre-teen boys. Counting to two for an eye poke, replicating a playful slap or doing the Curly Shuffle was the all the rage on every American playground in those days.

Recently, while in an introspective mood, I began to wonder why it is that men are so drawn to these masters of mayhem. And, just like that, it came to me:

Men like to see other men fail.

CONSIDER THE FACTS:
- THE STOOGES HAD NO GIRLFRIENDS.
- THEY HAD NO STEADY EMPLOYMENT.
- THEIR CLOTHES DIDN'T QUITE FIT.
- THEY WERE FIRED FROM NEARLY EVERY JOB THEY HAD.
- AND THEY WERE INEPT IN ANY ENDEAVOR THEY UNDERTOOK.

Fed up with their husbands' Stoogey ways, three ladies exact their revenge. *In the Sweet Pie and Pie* **(Columbia Pictures, 1941).**
COURTESY OF C3 ENTERTAINMENT, INC.

In other words, they were losers. And no matter how bad a man's life is, the Stooges are always there to elevate and stroke his ego.

FAMILY TIES

My great-uncle, Carl Lertzman, had left his hometown of Cleveland, Ohio, to find "fame and fortune" in Hollywood. Although he never found fortune, he briefly found fame. In 1964 — the year of the Beatles' British Invasion — he and his own rock group (The Bo Weevils) had a hit single with the novelty tune, "The Beetles Gonna Getcha." Besides being a "One-Hit Wonder," he had owned and operated Lertzman Electric and Appliance on Hollywood Boulevard at Western Avenue. As luck would have it, this was in close proximity to the Los Feliz area where Larry Fine lived. Larry and his wife Mabel, in fact, were two of his biggest customers. They would eventually bring Moe and Helen Howard

The Stooges give special attention to an ingénue on the set of *Baby Sitter Jitters* (Columbia Pictures, 1951). COURTESY OF C3 ENTERTAINMENT, INC.

to the store and they too would become regular patrons. Moe, Larry, Shemp and Curly all bought their first television sets from Lertzman Electric and Appliance.

According to Uncle Carl, Larry was always short of cash and had a rather large charge account that was in arrears. Carl, though, never forced the issue. Perhaps out of appreciation for this courtesy, Larry would invite Carl to bring any of his out-of-town visitors to the soundstages at Columbia where the Stooges filmed their shorts. Once admitted into the studio gates, Carl was treated like a VIP. Larry and Mabel eventually made good on their tab, and the three became friends. Carl also developed a friendship with Moe and Helen. Moe, Larry and Shemp were even guests at his daughter's wedding.

In June of 1950 my dad, Ron Lertzman, decided to pay a visit to Los Angeles, where he was planning to attend school. Uncle Carl was always bragging that he rubbed elbows with Hollywood stars and that if Dad ever came to visit, he would personally introduce him to each and every one. On the train ride from Cleveland to Los Angeles, Dad daydreamed of the screen idols he was about to

**The original "Wedding Crashers" — Shemp, Larry and Moe. The bride
herself (Marcia Lertzman) recalls that "my Uncle Carl was going to sing
and the boys came up to stop him." Los Angeles, California, 1950.**
COURTESY OF DAVID LERTZMAN

encounter: Gary Cooper . . . Clark Gable . . . Spencer Tracy. This,
he told himself, was going to be quite an experience.

How disappointed he was when the only "stars" he met were the
Three Stooges.

> "To me, they were the bottom of the barrel in
> films and no one in Cleveland was ever going to
> be impressed that I met them," my dad told me
> very recently. "They were just three very short
> Jews [we are also Jewish]. Don't get me wrong —
> they were very sweet men, but they weren't my
> idea of movie stars. They were more like my two
> uncles who ran a deli in Cleveland — only not as
> funny.

"For the next three days, I trekked down from my Uncle's house in the valley to the Columbia stages in a rundown area on Gower Street and watched the boys rehearse and shoot their scenes [for a short called *Baby Sitter Jitters*, released in February 1951]. I remember that it was swelteringly hot and they had a lot of big fans running. Larry was usually sitting next to a radio, listening to the horse races. Moe was the taskmaster, constantly yelling at Larry to come back to rehearsal. During the long breaks, they would have a card table set up just outside of the soundstage where they would play cards with each other and some of the stagehands. They would ask me to join them while they played either poker or gin rummy. I did join them a few times, but Moe was constantly bickering with Larry. Shemp was probably the nicest to me and he would constantly be teasing me about my height [I'm six-one].

"I watched them film a scene with a little boy [David Windsor]. To make him cry, they put some drops in his eyes. I think the kid was more upset at having drops forced into his eyes rather than the actual drops and he naturally began to get irate and went into a crying jag. I remember that Shemp began talking and kidding around with the little boy after the scene, trying to get a laugh out of him. The director was a rather tall and very crude guy [Jules White]. When the boys asked me to appear as an extra in a scene, this director let out a tirade of obscenities at them. I remember Moe walked away from him, just nodding his head. Actually, they seemed quite frightened of this director. As a matter of fact, I never did get the opportunity to be an extra on the film.

"I *did* enjoy wandering around the Columbia lot where I got a chance to meet Jean Arthur and Judy Holiday at the commissary (at different times). After those three memorable days on the lot, I decided to explore the rest of Los Angeles, which was really fascinating. I also had dinner at Uncle Carl's house with Larry and Mabel Fine. I remember that both of them had drunk quite a bit and left Carl's highly inebriated. In fact, I drove them home in Carl's car to their apartment at the Hotel Knickerbocker."

Not surprisingly, I've had my father tell and retell that story to me again and again and again.

A New Era

A generation passed since my father's memorable trip to Hollywood. It was now June of 1973. I was a seventeen-year-old with an ambition. I told my parents that I wanted to take a trip to Los Angeles to search out potential colleges. UCLA and USC, I explained, would receive an especially hard look. In truth, this was only a subterfuge. I had no intention of attending either school. I just wanted to be in the same state as Moe and Larry.

Through my connection to Uncle Carl, I was able to wangle an invitation to Moe's house for lunch. I remember the day as though it were yesterday. I arrived at his residence (on Thrasher, in the hills above Sunset) around one o'clock in the afternoon. As I rang the front doorbell, I noticed the manicured lawn and garden; I later learned that Moe himself tended the flowers and plants. A small woman answered the door: It was Mrs. Howard — or Helen, as she introduced herself. She graciously invited me inside the house. It was beautifully appointed, with everything in its proper place. As I was taking in the ambiance, I saw *him*. It was Moe, of course, although not the Moe I knew from the shorts. At seventy-six, he was thin and rather fragile. He was dressed casually, in a pastel sweater and checkered pants. The familiar bowl haircut was not present; his thick, white hair was neatly combed back. What struck me most was his size — or lack thereof. Dad was right: He really is short, I thought — not quite five-feet tall. To me, however, he was a giant. Of comedy.

Moe was a bit reserved — formal; even standoffish. In my zeal to impress him with my years of Stooge study, I found myself spouting facts about his career. It worked. The more I talked, the friendlier he became.

I was shown on a tour of the house, but what I remember most is Moe's office, which was filled with colorful memorabilia. Record album jackets bearing the Stooges' images were proudly displayed on the wall.

It was a beautiful summer's day and Moe decided he wanted lunch on the backyard patio. Helen immediately went to work in the kitchen.

We sat together at a glass table, talking about anything and everything related to the Stooges. What impressed me — and does so to this day — was the man's innate humility. I got the distinct impression that Moe did not consider himself to be an artist in the sense that many of his contemporaries had been. He thought of himself and most of his fellow Stooges as second-rate vaudevillians and low-echelon movie comics. He did not consider himself in the same class as Abbott and Costello or Laurel and Hardy or the Marx Brothers or even the Ritz Brothers.

Now the fellow who invented the Stooges — *he* had been truly great.

Ted Healy, Moe felt, was the draw when they played in vaudeville, not the Stooges. He alone was the reason their act played only the top-rung circuits. But Healy's alcoholism made it all but impossible to work for the man. When Moe, Larry and Curly left his employ and became the Three Stooges, Healy turned vindictive. He even threatened to blow up a theater during one of their live engagements.

Healy had volatile relationships with almost everyone in his inner circle, including his wife Betty. She was understandably upset by his frequent infidelities with chorus girls and she was anything but stoic about this. Once, in the Stooges' presence, she took a shot at him, and the bullet grazed his head.

"Healy was bald; that's why he always wore that fedora," Moe told me. "That day it saved his life. Lucky for him he had his hat on."

Moe and Larry feared Healy, it is true. They also retained a modicum of affection for him, at least when he was sober. Shemp, on the other hand, hated his former boyhood friend. More than once, the normally gentle Shemp told Moe that he wanted to kill Ted Healy. This stemmed from being on the receiving end of Healy's ferocious onstage slaps. These slaps had to be wallops, the boisterous comic explained: "They gotta be heard in the back of the house."

While the audience howled with raucous delight, Shemp's head reeled from the pain. After one slap too many, he quit the act and pursued a solo career in movies.

Enter Jerry Howard — "Babe" to friends and family. He had been doing a hilarious act with a bandleader in New York. In order to fit in with the Stooges, he had to have a distinctive look, something that made him stand out in a grotesque manner. Moe had the bowl haircut, Larry the frizzy hair, but Jerry's hair was long and wavy. He was almost attractive, and Stooges weren't meant to be attractive. So he volunteered to shave not only his head but also his handlebar mustache.

And "Curly" was born.

There's a term used by old-time comics to describe someone who has the gift: Funny Bones. Shemp had those. He was not only a fine physical comedian, he was a great storyteller — a raconteur, if you will. But Curly's brilliance went beyond the Funny Bones description. He had an instinctual feel for comedy that was almost scary, he was so good. Nothing in comedy is completely original, however, and Moe believes Curly had been influenced by a once-famous comic named Hugh Herbert, a stocky little man whose catch phrase was "Hoo-Hoo-Hoo!" (Curly's, of course, is "Woo-Woo-Woo!"). According to Moe, Curly later served as an influence for Lou Costello. He saw Costello backstage at some of their early performances, intently studying Curly's mannerisms. Some of these later ended up in the Abbott and Costello features.

Moe admired his brother's talent enormously, and was fiercely protective of him. He never used the word, but Curly (or Babe, as he called him) was almost a Savant Idiot. Offscreen, he was virtually incapable of taking care of himself. So Moe took it upon himself to look after him, setting him up in several different houses over the years. He did the same thing with Larry, he told me.

"How is Larry doing these days?" I asked.

"He had a stroke a few years ago," Moe said. "They've got him over at the [Motion Picture] Home. You wanna go see him?"

I could hardly say "Yes" fast enough.

"We'll go right after lunch," he said.

OLD FRIENDS

Moe and I climbed into Helen's Cadillac and made the short trip to Woodland Hills (It was all side streets; I don't think we ever even got on the freeway). Moe was driving and behind the wheel he looked like a little kid who could barely see over the dashboard. It was quite an image.

We entered the building known as the Lodge and walked unannounced into Larry's private room. Given his recent stroke, I was prepared to see a faded version of the famous "Stooge in the Middle," but I was still surprised when I saw him.

Surprised and saddened.

Replacing the adept clown with the frizzy hair was an old man, shriveled up in a wheelchair.

Moe greeted his partner in Yiddish: "*Vi gaits?* (What's doing?)"

"*Gornish* (Nothing)," Larry responded.

"This is Carl Lertzman's nephew," Moe said by way of introduction.

Larry lit up. "How is old Carl?" he asked. "How's his recording career goin'?"

Moe wheeled Larry outdoors to a garden area and the three of us sat and talked. Sometimes the conversation between the two degenerated into a quasi-argument. It was never over anything serious — it was just the way they communicated, as my father had witnessed twenty years earlier. Some of the arguments resulted from Moe's dismissive attitude toward Larry's opinions. I got the distinct impression that Moe felt a bit superior to his partner. Moe had been the team's leader, after all. He had been the better businessman of the two, and he had the money to prove it. Shrewd investments in

This signed publicity photo taken on the set of *Woman Haters* (Columbia Pictures, 1934) was given to Carl Lertzman by his friends, Curly, Moe and Larry. COURTESY OF DAVID LERTZMAN

California real estate were said to be the foundation of his fortune. He inherited this knack for business from his dynamo of a mother, who had been a realtor in Brooklyn, New York. Larry, of course, was not a Howard (originally Horowitz) and such acumen did not come naturally to him. He had spent his money as fast as he could earn it. For him, life was a cabaret, as the song says. Now, at seventy, he was old and sick — and broke. He was also tired. In the middle of one of Moe's stories, Larry nodded off. Moe looked at me and rolled his eyes.

"*Oy*" he said under his breath.

As I watched these two ex-Stooges together, I was struck by their easy rapport. In a word, it can best be described as "comfortable." By that time, they had known each other for almost fifty years. They knew each other backwards and forwards. They had traveled across the country with each other. They were brothers. They were not related by blood, but they were brothers.

THE END OF AN ERA

Within a short span of time, they were both gone. Larry and Moe died within four months of each other in 1975.

At that time there were only a handful of reliable books on the Golden Age of Comedy, and these — as I have said — were written by Leonard Maltin. Through my good friends, film professors John Sonneborn and Marty Davis, I traded 16mm prints with Mr. Maltin and discussed the Stooges with him. After hearing about my encounters, he encouraged me to write my own book. It was an idea I had originally broached with Moe. ("Who would care?" he said.) Up until the time of his death, Moe had been slaving away on his memoirs, but he had little hope of ever having them published. Apparently, he had shopped the idea around and encountered a series of polite rejections. I was concerned about the same fate for my project, but Mr. Maltin generously recommended me to his publisher. Through a literary agent, I contacted a representative from Crown Publishers in New York. They were interested.

I was then auditing a course at Cal Northridge. The subject was comedy and the instructor was none other than the legendary Lucille Ball. Everyone in the class wanted to talk to her about *I Love Lucy*, but I was only interested in her co-starring role in the 1934 Stooges short, *Three Little Pigskins*. In a moment of inspiration, I asked her if she would consider writing the foreword to my book-in-progress.

Her face fell. Unconsciously flicking a cigarette ash at me, she said in that deep, smoke-tainted voice, "For those three midgets? Forget it!"

So much for that idea . . .

In 1977 the pictorial biography *Moe Howard and the 3 Stooges* was published by Citadel Press. It is a fitting tribute to a great career. With that publication came the dissolution of my own project. The stories were told, the pictures were laid out — it was done. I had no idea then that products based on the Stooges' lives and likenesses would become a veritable cottage industry for decades to come.

I'm grateful to finally have this opportunity to share my memories

Larry and Lucille Ball (before she became America's favorite redhead) in a publicity still for *Three Little Pigskins* (Columbia Pictures, 1934).
COURTESY OF C3 ENTERTAINMENT, INC.

of my favorite comedy team. They continue to bring me joy to the present day.

Now if I could just make my wife a convert . . .

RICK LERTZMAN WAS THE CEO OF HIS FAMILY-RUN BUSINESS LIQUIDATION FIRM FOR TWENTY-FIVE YEARS. HE WAS ALSO THE EDITOR AND PUBLISHER OF *FILM WORLD MAGAZINE* IN THE EARLY EIGHTIES. AN INVETERATE MULTI-TASKER, HE IS CURRENTLY COMPILING BOOKS ON BOB CUMMINGS, MAX JACOBSON ("DR. FEELGOOD"), PAUL HENNING (WITH LINDA KAYE HENNING) AND ABBOTT AND COSTELLO. A NATIVE OF CLEVELAND, OHIO, RICK AND HIS WIFE SANDY DEDICATE WHAT FREE TIME THEY HAVE TO RESCUE WORK WITH ANIMALS.

MICRO-PHONIES: MOE AND LARRY ON THE RADIO

BY ED BUSCH

Today, with cable and the Internet, classic stars from the Golden Age of Television are everywhere. But during the 1970s syndication was a fairly new phenomenon, one that was not particularly watched or followed. A lot of the old shows and stars just disappeared from view. Even though they were somewhat out of favor during that time, they remained interesting to me. I loved their work and loved their programs. And that's how I came to interview such television icons as Adam West and Burt Ward (*Batman and Robin*), Jerry Mathers (*Leave it to Beaver*) and DeForest Kelly (*Star Trek*). Then, on September 27, 1974, I had the opportunity to conduct telephone interviews with two of my all-time favorites: Moe Howard and Larry Fine of the Three Stooges. I grew up loving their films, so it was an honor to talk with them. The interviews had been arranged by Bob Bernet of Dallas. Bob had the foresight to tape-record the original broadcasts, and I am reprinting a condensed (and reorganized) version of my conversations with Larry and Moe here for the first time.*

---

* If you would like to hear the complete interviews, you can do so by ordering a copy of Bob Bernet's CD, *My Pal Moe* (http://web2.airmail.net/willdogs/).

Talking With Larry

Ed: Hello, Larry. This is Ed Busch at WFAA Radio in Dallas, Texas.

Larry: Oh, yes.

Ed: How are you doing?

Larry: Pretty good.

Ed: Alright. I do a talk show here in Dallas and a number of people suggested that I give you a call and say hello. So . . . Hello!

Larry: Hello.

Ed: (laughs) I was gonna do "Woo Woo Woo Woo!"

Larry: Curly.

Ed: Yeah, that's Curly. I don't do too good of a job, but I certainly have seen every one of the Three Stooges episodes, Larry, I believe five . . . six times. I'd like to ask you some questions about your career, if you don't mind.

Larry: Go ahead.

Ed: Do you have much of a relationship with Moe Howard these days?

Larry: I sure do. Yes.

Ed: We're gonna call Moe later on this evening . . . to say hello.

Larry: Are you sure he's home?

ED: We already checked it out. He's gonna be waiting for our call a little later on tonight.

LARRY: Oh, I see.

ED: Now how long ago, Larry, did you start filming the Three Stooges comedies?

LARRY: The comedies that we made ourselves started in Nineteen-thirty-four . . . We made 'em clear through Nineteen-fifty-eight.

ED: So, twenty-four years.

LARRY: Consecutive, yes.

ED: How popular were the Three Stooges comedies in that twenty-four year span?

LARRY: Well, I guess, from what we understood, nobody could book any of the Stooges pictures unless they took the other eight comedies of Columbia. That's kind of a hold-up thing — you know what I mean?

ED: But your comedy was so strong that they couldn't get any of the other ones?

LARRY: They had to take a series of eight.

ED: So, yours was kind of like the Cadillac of comedy shows.

LARRY: I think so.

ED: In all the antics you did in the Three Stooges, were you ever injured? Did you break any bones or anything?

LARRY: We never broke bones. We did get hurt, but never serious.

ED: In all those years of fooling around?

LARRY: No. We were really lucky.

ED: Huh! (Laughs). Now you went through . . . was it three or four Curly's?

LARRY: Well, we started originally, you know, with Shemp, Moe and I.

ED: Oh, he was the first?

LARRY: Yeah. Then Shemp stayed in New York. We came out here and brought Curly. He got sick in 'forty-six and Shemp came back with us and stayed. Curly died in 'fifty-two. Shemp died in 'fifty-five. Then we got Joe Besser in 'fifty-six for two or three years. Then from 'fifty-eight till Nineteen-seventy (when I got sick), we got Joe DeRita.

ED: So, that's four guys.

LARRY: Yeah.

ED: But you and Moe were the hearty guys. You went through it all.

LARRY: Yeah.

ED: Do people call or write you much anymore?

LARRY: I get hundreds of letters a week.

ED: No kidding?

LARRY: Yeah, well I get a lot of publicity in this place [The Motion Picture Country Home]. I'm sure that's why I get letters.

ED: Would you mind if some people from Texas wrote you a letter?

LARRY: I sure would not.

ED: Alright. Let me get an address for you . . . in fact I think I wrote it down here. Motion Picture Country House, Woodland Hills, right?

LARRY: Right.

ED: And the zip is 91364.

LARRY: Right. But the exact address is 23388 Mulholland Drive.

ED: Mul-holland-Drive. Where's that? Is it near Los Angeles?

LARRY: Well, it's about . . . I'd say it's about fourteen miles from Hollywood.

ED: Oh, so you're very close.

LARRY: Yeah.

ED: Now you had a stroke recently. How are you feeling?

LARRY: Well, they tell me I'm doing very good.

ED: Right. I assume you are hopeful of being able to walk again?

LARRY: Yeah, well I do now with what they call a four-pronged cane.

ED: Are you surprised, Larry, that the Three Stooges and all those hundreds of comedies you made are still so very popular today?

LARRY: I'm amazed . . . because that's a good forty years. To think that they are still popular and getting bigger every day!

ED: Right. Do you ever watch those anymore?

LARRY: Well, out here, we don't get it . . . You need a cable. We have a cable at my daughter's house, where I spend a lot of time on my weekends. And I see 'em then.

ED: What do you think when watching the films?

LARRY: I'm too critical of myself.

ED: Oh, really?

LARRY: Yeah.

ED: You don't think your performances were so great at times?

LARRY: I don't like it.

ED: Did you closely follow a script or did you guys just kind of mess around?

LARRY: No, we fooled around because if it wasn't funny they would cut it out.

ED: Oh, so you did a lot of filming and edited out . . . edited in the parts you liked?

LARRY: They'd let it run, and then cut out what they didn't like.

ED: Oh. Is there any particular thing that you like best that you did? Was it the pie throwing? You guys sawed each other in half . . . I mean, you did so many things to each other . . .

LARRY: Well, I think that Moe was dynamite with that poking in the eyes.

ED: Oh, yeah.

LARRY: He got very close and never hurt anybody.

ED: When he stuck his two fingers into your eyes, but he never quite touched you.

LARRY: No. He had a beautiful touch. He could have been a pickpocket.

ED: (laughs) Maybe he was, Larry.

LARRY: I don't know . . . he's pretty wealthy.

ED: Is he?

LARRY: Yes he is.

ED: Did he invest his money or what?

LARRY: Yes. In real estate.

ED: Ahhhh.

LARRY: He owns a lot of North Hollywood.

ED: (laughs) He owns a lot of North Hollywood?

LARRY: Yeah.

ED: Wow. Well, you guys, over a period of time, must have made quite a deal of money, huh?

LARRY: Yes, but he knew what to do with it.

ED: What did you do? Spend it?

LARRY: Yes, I did.

ED: Well, I think you had a good idea, too. That's a good thing to do with money — spend it.

LARRY: Well, I know . . . .especially . . . luckily I did it when I was young, because I'm not in the position to spend it now.

ED: Well, I know you have a lot of other things to do and I have to make some other calls, too. Let me give the address again. And I'd love for the people listening to drop you a line and say hello and perhaps we can call again a little later on, alright?

LARRY: Okay. Anytime.

ED: And I'll betcha there's a lot of people listening in the Southwest, Larry, that'll drop you a line and just say hello.

LARRY: Well, they'd be perfectly welcome. If anybody writes, I'll send a picture.

ED: Hey, that's great! Thank you, Larry, and have a nice night.

LARRY: Okay, Ed.

ED: Goodnight.

LARRY: Goodnight.

ED: Bye-bye. (Ends call) Wow. Isn't he a nice fella? Larry Fine.

AND TALKING WITH MOE

MOE: Hello?

EB: Hi. This is Ed Busch of WFAA in Dallas.

MOE: Oh. How are ya?

EB: How are you doing? Were you expecting my call? I think someone gave you a call this afternoon that I might be calling?

MOE: Yeah.

EB: Bob [Bernet].

MOE: Yeah, he called.

EB: And I do a talk show here and so many people have such interest about you fellas. In fact, we just talked with Larry last hour on the show . . .

MOE: Yeah . . .

EB: . . . and he gave us a little bit of background on the Three Stooges and I wonder if we could talk to you for a few minutes.

MOE: I guess so. Why not?

EB: Alright . . . well, the one thing that I heard that was amazing and I saw you, I think, on Mike Douglas a short time ago . . . you're seventy-seven years old!

MOE: Four months past.

EB: When did you first think of doing comedy professionally, Moe?

MOE: Well, I didn't do comedy until Nineteen-twenty-two. Originally, I did all dramatic work in dramatic stock companies. I was on a showboat up and down the Mississippi River for two years. And I played dramatic roles mostly. But, beginning in Nineteen-twenty-two, I started doing comedy. I enjoyed doing it. I could go right back to dramatic works without any difficulty.

EB: We were talking with Larry about the original series and someone called up so let me start off with this . . . when you guys went out to California to start filming the original Three Stooges comedies, what were you doing in the East? Did you have a comedy act?

MOE: Oh, yes.

EB: In what? Vaudeville?

MOE: Oh, yes, yes. Vaudeville. Plus, the first trip we moved to California to do a picture with . . . we did one for Fox — *Soup to Nuts.* It was written by Rube Goldberg, the cartoonist.

EB: The guy who made all the wild inventions.

MOE: Yeah.

EB: And that was the first movie you did?

MOE: That was the first one in talkie movies.

EB: You did some silents?

MOE: I made . . . I made films in the old silent days many, many years ago.

EB: I guess in New York or on the East Coast it was you — Moe Howard, Larry Fine and your brother Shemp, right?

MOE: Right. That's the original three.

EB: Okay, now in vaudeville, would you do the same kind of stuff you did later in the movies?

MOE: Somewhat, only not on such a large scale.

EB: Now, who came up with the idea for the haircuts — especially yours?

MOE: Well, this wasn't just an idea, but the haircut was born in a very odd way. I was the fourth boy in a family of five boys. And I was supposed to be the girl.

EB: (Laughs)

MOE: In fact, my mother used to wake me up about twenty minutes before the rest, to go to school, and she used to make those finger curls on my head. Until I was about eleven years old I wore curls almost down to my shoulders.

EB: Oh, really?

MOE: I had to fight my way to school, in school and back home from school.

EB: Didn't you wonder why you were a little different?

MOE: No. No. I knew my mother wanted it that way and I wasn't going to bust up her thoughts, you know.

EB: Okay.

MOE: But, finally, I did it. In other words, when I met some fella that was taller than I or older than I and would give me that sissy routine, then I had a friend called

Rusty Johnson. We'd stand back to back and fight 'em off. His mother got tired of having him come home with black eyes and a tooth knocked out occasionally. She said that she didn't want him to go with me anymore. So, he said, "Look, if you want me for a friend anymore, we gotta do something about those curls." So I got a hold of his mother's scissors and without looking — I cut the job right off all the way around. When I looked in the mirror, that's what it looked like with the haircut.

EB: And you kept it all that time?

MOE: I kept it all that time.

EB: What did your mother say?

MOE: She kinda was good about it . . . because first of all, I was afraid to go home. I hid under the porch. We had a summer porch underneath with latticework around, you know? I hid under there till about two in the morning 'cause I heard my mother say, "You better call the police."

EB: To look for you.

MOE: Yeah..and then I started coughing lightly, you know . . . and then I made the coughs a little louder. Then my father said, "Uh oh. There he is under the porch." Then they pulled me out with a rake . . .

EB: (Laughs)

MOE: They got me inside and my mother took one look at me and said, "I knew it was going to happen sometime and I'm happy it happened."

EB: Wow. So you hid for nothing.

MOE: Yeah.

EB: So, you just kept it (the haircut) into show business.

MOE: That's right.

EB: How would you describe it? Kind of a . . . Beatle haircut?

MOE: Nooooo. Of course, you're putting the Beatles in there . . . .they weren't even born at the time.

EB: I agree, but I'm trying to compare it to what was supposedly a revolution in the mid-sixties, Moe Howard was wearing in the 'twenties or 'thirties.

MOE: Yeah, well this is sort of a bedpan haircut. You know, the baby's potty used to be under the bed.

EB: Oh, yeah.

MOE: You put that on your head and cut around it.

EB: (Laughs) So, you had the haircut and you kept it in show business. Your act, in vaudeville, Moe . . . was it mostly slapstick?

MOE: It was, but there were a lot funny jokes in between. We found that action was very important. And the tempo is fast.

EB: Right.

MOE: So, if they lost the joke, we'd still cover it up with some kind of thunk on the head or a hit in the stomach or something.

EB: Right. Oh, Larry said to tell you . . . that he mentioned that you were at your best with your two fingers to poke someone in the eye because you never touched them.

MOE: That's right. I never went off line with it.

EB: Boy, I tell you, I've seen all of your movies five times, Moe, and for the world, it looks like you're poking the guy right in the eye.

MOE: Oh, yes. They had a great sense of how to take it by throwing the head back. Larry found a joke there. He'd cover his eyes and say, "I can't see! I can't see!" I'd say, "What's the matter?" He'd say, "I got my eyes closed."

EB: (Laughs) Oh, yeah. He also did one where he held his finger in his eye and he'd say, "I got something in my eye! I've got something in my eye!" And you'd say, "What's that?" And he'd say, "I got my finger."

MOE: Yeah.

EB: And then you'd punch him, right?

MOE: Yeah.

EB: How is it that you became the leader of the three?

MOE: Because I was too smart for them.

EB: (laughs)

MOE: No. No. I don't know. I just happened to be . . . it started when I used to do their income tax for them. And anytime there was something to do, one of would say, "Oh, Moe will take care of it." And I did.

EB: So, you made the first movie, *Soup to Nuts*. Was that a
        big success?

MOE: Yes. It was quite a good picture. From there we went to
        MGM for a year. And we made five two-reel comedies
        and four feature-length pictures. A feature-length picture
        called *Dancing Lady* with Joan Crawford and Clark
        Gable . . . *Fugitive Lovers*, with Robert Montgomery
        and Madge Evans. Made one called *Meet the Baron*,
        with Jimmy Durante and Jack Pearl. And made one
        with Lee Tracy called, *Turn Back the Clock*. And one
        called *Hollywood Party* which was an all-star picture.

EB: Did those do well?

MOE: Well, yes. They did very well at the time. Two of them
        were in color. The comedies were in color.

EB: In the mid-thirties?

MOE: Yessir.

EB: Boy, those must have been important movies then.

MOE: Yes they were. I'll tell you how it was. Not that we
        made them, but . . . they had a few big musicals that
        MGM had . . . and they were too long, so they cut
        two musicals out. And we wrote a short around one
        musical — a color musical and added some stuff to it
        and made a short out of it. We did two of them like that.

EB: Using the available footage.

MOE: That's right.

EB: Now when you, I guess you left there again, right?
        In 'thirty-four you started making the comedies for
        Columbia Pictures.

MOE: That's right. We left in uh . . . let me see . . . in April of Nineteen hundred and thirty-four and we opened up at Columbia in June of Nineteen-thirty-four.

EB: Now, were you at that time, Moe, already the Three Stooges? Were they one of the top groups in America then?

MOE: I'll tell you what the sequence was. All those comedies were made for the theater, you see.

EB: Right.

MOE: . . . we reached a very fine peak in that element, then the theaters in the South and the Midwest started doing double-features which cut the comedy out — started to drop away until Columbia released the pictures on TV. Then it really went sky-high.

EB: You mean you had more popularity on TV than you did on the screen?

MOE: Oh, yes. Oh, certainly. You couldn't get a five-year-old kid into the theater and have him enjoy anything. So you can see the advantage of television. Because the youngsters at home . . . our pictures are the finest babysitters in the country.

EB: Were these very big productions? I seem to recall seeing the credits on television that there were very few names mentioned.

MOE: There were several that were mentioned in practically every one of them.

EB: Right.

MOE: Vernon Dent, Buddy Jamison, Phil Van Zandt, Emil Sitka —

EB: You had one guy, and I'm sorry I can't remember his name. He was a heavyset tall fellow. He was in that Nazi movie you talked about and he played the police chief and a judge . . .

MOE: Yeah, well, that's Vernon Dent.

EB: Is he still around?

MOE: No, he passed away. And then there was Bud Jamison, another one was with in a bunch of pictures. He passed away. Phil Van Zandt was one of the good ones we had. He passed away. The only living ones that were with us over a number of our comedies was Emil Sitka, he's still around working around. And Christine McIntire, the beautiful blonde with the wonderful singing voice. Great performer. She's not working anymore. She's married and happily married and is out of the business. She's alive and kicking.

EB: On your set, was it a lot of fun and games or was it down to business?

MOE: Ahhh, yes. A lot of fun.

EB: You guys really enjoyed what you did.

MOE: Oh, yes. Everybody on the set enjoyed . . . we always played little pranks and things like that.

EB: Would you sometimes throw a pie at someone else instead of who you're supposed to?

MOE: No. No. Like we'd . . . in those director's chairs, one of the cast would sit in the director's chair and we'd take a cigarette lighter and light the thing underneath just until it got hot then they'd jump up . . . like a cannon.

EB: One of the things that I noticed, and maybe it was just me, because I'm such a devotee, but when you would, not you, but when your director, would learn a camera technique, such as . . . one of them seem to be throwing a pie . . . they learned to throw the pie into the camera. Throwing a knife. They started throwing a knife into the camera. They would do almost the whole movie . . .

MOE: No. That was in 3-D.

EB: Oh, was that it?

MOE: That's what it was.

EB: Oh, no kidding! 3-D Three Stooges?

MOE: Yeah, and I'll tell you something else. Any pie that you saw hitting someone else outside of me — I threw it.

EB: Oh, even off camera.

MOE: Yeah, I have saved the studio, by word of mouth; I have saved the studio thousands of dollars in time. And time was money.

EB: Right, because of film costs and so forth.

MOE: By my accuracy with the pies.

EB: Because you didn't miss.

MOE: Right. Because if you threw at a woman and you hit her hair instead of her face, there was a shampoo and twenty minutes under a dryer. If you hit her dress, there was a change of wardrobe and the whole thing. All that time.

EB: Wow. Yeah, I never thought about that.

MOE: Never missed.

EB: What were those pies made out of, Moe?

MOE: (laughs) We used to have a big pot. Oh, it was about a twenty-gallon pot. And in there we mixed granulated pumpkin, you know, ground pumpkin?

EB: Yeah.

MOE: And we used flour, whipped cream, chocolate syrup and blueberries.

EB: (laughs) So, it simply wasn't shaving cream.

MOE: No. No, no. You see, if you used regular pies like they make in the store and things like that, it would hit the face and fly off.

EB: Right.

MOE: But what we made, it hit and stuck.

EB: And splattered.

MOE: Splattered and covered the whole face.

EB: Did you just kind of follow a story outline or was a lot of it scripted?

MOE: No. There was basically a story.

EB: I see.

MOE: We used to write a nine-page what we called a "treatment." In other words, a layman's word would be an outline.

EB: Right.

MOE: And we would turn that over to two of the finest screenplay writers in the business — that we had — one was Felix Adler . . .

EB: Oh, yeah, another name I remember.

MOE: He used to do all the [intertitles] in the silent pictures for Chaplin and others. The other was Clyde Bruckman, who was the writer for Harold Lloyd.

EB: Right.

MOE: So we would give them the treatment and they would do a first draft of the script . . . twenty-nine pages from the nine-page treatment.

EB: Right.

MOE: Then, we'd get it back and make a second draft because most of the time they would have the wrong person saying the wrong words. You couldn't have Larry or Curly use any rough or tough talk to me.

EB: Right, because you were supposed to be the rough guy.

MOE: Yeah. So, I would place the dialogue where it belonged and then we'd make the final draft.

EB: How long would that be then?

MOE: Oh, this pre-production with the storyline ready for shooting would take about three weeks.

EB: And how many pages of script then?

MOE: Twenty-nine.

MOE: Then it would take about three days to do a picture.

EB: Is that very full like six in the morning till six at night?

MOE: Oh, no, no, no, no. No, we'd start at eight-thirty in the morning and finish up about five-thirty.

EB: Almost business hours.

MOE: Yes. You see, we never rehearsed. You couldn't rehearse because you'd lose the spontaneity.

EB: You just went ahead and did it. How long would the film run?

MOE: The early ones ran eighteen minutes and then later on we were cut down to fifteen.

EB: Yeah, I don't think they pushed Moe around.

MOE: You'd have a dead director on your hands if they pushed us around.

EB: You guys were "biggies."

MOE: It wasn't a question of "biggies." First of all, the directors that we worked with depended a lot on us because they didn't understand us truly, because you couldn't put our type of work into words and make it sound funny because it wasn't funny talking about it. It was only funny in the action that you did. In other words, a director would depend on his performers. A good director never told you what to do. He told you what NOT to do. If he found something, he'd say, "Hey, Moe. I don't think you ought to do that piece

over there because it's so far back from the camera,
they won't realize what you're doing anyhow. Those are
the way those things operate because if they said, "Hey,
don't do that . . . anything like that!" well, we'd just
foul the picture up, that's all.

EB: A mother called me between when I talked with Larry
Fine and talked with you tonight. She said, "Would
you please ask Moe if there was a problem with kids
imitating the Three Stooges actions" because she has a
problem with her six-year-old wanting to go around
poking people in the eyes.

MOE: Let me tell you . . . there's a great answer to that.
There was a great psychologist . . . a woman
psychologist . . . when some Parent Teachers
Association in Cleveland asked the station . . . telling
the station that we were too rough for the kids.

EB: Right.

MOE: Some of them were copying what the boys did. So,
the station took it up with this child psychologist
and said did she think that anything that the Stooges
did would bear on the doings of the youngsters. And
she said, "The only time that will happen is if the
child who does that is a problem child and would
be a problem child if he never saw the Stooges."
You see?

EB: Right. So are you going to be doing any personal
appearances, Moe?

MOE: Just came back from appearing at the University of
Buffalo in New York.

EB: Oh, you're making the rounds, then. What are the
university kids saying to you, Moe? I assume that

you have some question and answer sessions, right?

MOE: Yes. They wrote out cards so there wouldn't be bedlam in the audience.

EB: (laughs) What kind of things are they interested in?

MOE: Oh, they want to know how many pictures we made; how did we get into the business; where did the haircuts come from . . .

EB: The same stuff I'm asking you. Any television work in the future, guesting and so forth?

MOE: At the first of the year, I'll probably be on Carson and Merv Griffin both. I've done the fourth Mike Douglas Show two weeks ago.

EB: Did you have a favorite third Stooge? I know in talking with Larry tonight, he said there were four Curly's or Curly-Joe's. Did you have a favorite that you thought worked best with you guys?

MOE: There was never, never and there never will be a Stooge as good as my kid brother, Curly . . . I just can't begin to express the little tricks that he had. You know, he was a hard study and when he'd forget his lines, he'd fall to the floor and spin around like a top until he remembered what he had to say, or he'd do backward kicks or he'd lay on his shoulder and crawl like a snake. We never knew what he was gonna do half the time. No, never, never another Curly. Shemp was good. Shemp was a different type of comic, but Shemp was very good. Then, of course, we had this fellow, Joe Besser. He was cute . . . nice, but he was only with us for three years then we got a hold of Curly-Joe . . . Joe DeRita in Nineteen-fifty-eight until Nineteen-seventy-one. He was clever. He came out of burlesque. He was a clever performer and he was funny, but not Curly. He wasn't Curly. Curly was really great.

EB: Well, Moe, I appreciate so much talking with you tonight on really no notice and so many people are interested in finding out what happened with the Three Stooges and what's happening with your life, I hope you don't mind if sometime in the future I can give you a call again and we could talk some more.

MOE: No, I don't mind. I don't mind. I enjoy talking to nice people.

EB: That's good. Thank you, Moe and we'll be in touch.

MOE: Okay.

EB: Goodnight.

MOE: Goodnight.

ED BUSCH IS AN AWARD-WINNING TELEVISION PRODUCER, WRITER AND INTERVIEWER. HE BEGAN HIS RADIO CAREER IN HIS HOMETOWN OF LINCOLN PARK, MICHIGAN, WHEN THE LOCAL DISC JOCKEY HAD A HEART ATTACK ON AIR. ED FILLED IN AND STAYED ON THE AIR FOR THE NEXT THIRTY YEARS, FIRST AS A DJ AND LATER A TALK RADIO HOST. HE ALSO WORKED AS THE PRODUCER/WRITER/VOICE, CREATING AUDIO NEWSLETTERS FOR SEVERAL LARGE COMMERCIAL FIRMS, AND WAS THE PRODUCER/WRITER/INTERVIEWER FOR BLACK HISTORY MONTH TELEVISION FEATURES IN DALLAS/FORT WORTH. NOW RETIRED, ED AND HIS WIFE SYDNEY RESIDE IN MABANK, TEXAS.

QUILL PENS AND CONTRACT PLAYERS

BY MARK EVANIER

A couple of times in the early seventies, I trucked out to the Motion Picture Country Home in Woodland Hills to visit Larry Fine. He welcomed company and a chance to tell his anecdotes, of which he had no more than about a dozen. No matter what you asked him, he told you the same twelve stories. In fact, the second time I was there, he told me one yarn three times. The question everyone apparently put to him was, "Did you ever get injured making those movies?" He'd developed a little five-minute monologue/reply that you'd hear if you asked him what time it was.

His favorite story involved a stunt in the 1948 short *Heavenly Daze*. He and Moe were trying to sell a pen that would write under whipped cream. The "pen" was in a blender which would go berserk, shooting out of the mixing bowl and landing, arrow-like, in Larry's forehead. To achieve this cinematic splendor, they attached a tin plate with a hole in the center to his forehead, and fastened to that a spring wire which was to direct the pen to the hole in the center of the plate. When the pen shot out of the mixing bowl, the prop man was to throw the pen attached to the wire at Larry's forehead, popping it into the center hole. At least, that was the idea. Upon seeing the plate Larry protested, saying that the hole was too large. No, no, they assured him, It would work exactly as planned.

It didn't quite turn out that way.

At the crucial moment, the prop man lobbed the pen . . . and darned if it didn't land dead-center in the Fine forehead. As scripted, Larry howled in pain but it wasn't acting. When he pulled the pen out, he was bleeding like one of those stuck pigs you hear so much about.

©COLUMBIA PICTURES, 1948

That was the story as Larry told it. And told it and told it and told it . . .

Repetitive though he was, he really was a fascinating guy. In 1973 his autobiography, *Stroke of Luck*, was published . . . and it really was a remarkable book. And talk about a rare collector's item! I once turned down $500 for my copy of what may well be the worst-written celebrity autobiography — ever. Its two distinctions are that . . .

(1) It probably holds the world's record for the most typographical errors in one volume and . . .

(2) You rarely see anyone unintentionally get so many of the details of his own life wrong.

The book is written in the first person, as if by Larry Fine. The cover, though, reads "by James Carone" and there's an author photo of Mr. Carone on the back of the dust jacket. I don't know who Mr. Carone is or was, other than that he seemed to believe that you should never write eight words in a row without inserting at least four commas. He even invented a whole new kind of punctuation where you put two or three commas in a row.

I'll tell you how bad it is. If it was about someone else, you'd read a few pages of it and say, "Who wrote this — one of *The Three Stooges?*"

What's really odd about it is that as per its title, the book tries to view the story of Larry's stroke — the one that put him in a hospital for the rest of his life and took away his ability to walk — as a *good* thing. I certainly understand trying to put a positive spin on bad news and admire the tenacity it takes to overcome as much as one can and live with the frustration. But the book is so clumsily authored that at times, it's like Larry's saying, "Thank God I had that stroke . . . best thing that ever happened to me . . . you oughta try it."

While out at the Motion Picture Home, Larry introduced me to other old actors, most notably a woman named Babe London. She was "the fat girl" in countless films, including *Go West* with Buster Keaton, *Our Wife* with Laurel & Hardy and *Scrambled Brains* with the Stooges. Ms. London was thrilled that I knew who she was and she'd try to hijack my visits with Larry, diverting the conversation to her dozen anecdotes, which Larry was thoroughly sick of hearing.

So I'd just sit there while she tried to tell me for the third time about being falsely accused of having an affair with Roscoe "Fatty" Arbuckle. Larry waited impatiently for her to finish so he could tell me for the fifth time about the quill pen.

Neither Babe nor Larry was much good for history beyond these oft-told tales. When I got to speak, which wasn't often, I'd ask something like, "What was Charley Chase like?" And since neither Babe nor Larry had a good Charley Chase story, they'd both say, "He was great." And then Babe would quickly start telling me the Fatty Arbuckle story again while Larry would try to interrupt and tell me one more time about the quill pen. Or if I asked something that actually did jog either's memory, it would suddenly turn into a scene from *The Sunshine Boys*:

"We had this contract player at Columbia named Tommy Blake . . . "

"Tommy Blake didn't work for Columbia. He was over at Republic."

"Like hell he was. I used to see him every time I drove on the lot at Columbia and I'd always say, 'Hi, Tommy!'"

"Well, I don't know who you were saying hello to at Columbia because Tommy Blake was at Republic. That's where I said hi to him."

"When did you ever work for Republic?"

"Did I ever tell you about the time I got a quill pen shot into my forehead?"

MARK EVANIER IS A TELEVISION WRITER AND EDITOR, AND HAS ALSO WRITTEN HUNDREDS OF COMIC BOOKS, INCLUDING GROO THE WANDERER, SCOOBY DOO, BLACKHAWK AND DNAGENTS. IN TV, HE WORKED FOR ALL THE MAJOR ANIMATION STUDIOS AND WROTE THE GARFIELD CARTOON SHOWS FOR EIGHT YEARS. HE LIVES IN LOS ANGELES AND ALSO ONLINE AT HIS WEBSITE, WWW.NEWSFROMME.COM.

SEARCHING OUT THE STOOGES

BY SCOTT H. REBOUL

In the early 1970s I was in high school, growing up in New Jersey, and watching the Three Stooges every day on the local Philadelphia station Channel 29. At that time, there was very little biographical information available about the Three Stooges — no *Stroke of Luck* — no *Moe Howard and the 3 Stooges* — no documentaries — and no Internet. The only thing out there was Leonard Maltin's *Movie Comedy Teams*, published in 1970, with an excellent chapter on the Stooges. Maltin's book stated that Curly and Shemp Howard had died in the 1950s, but it didn't provide much information on the current status of Moe Howard, Larry Fine, Joe Besser and Joe DeRita.

Since I hadn't seen the Stooges in anything new, I wondered if any of them were still living, and if they were, how old were they, what did they look like and why weren't they still making movies? These questions were frequently the topic of lunchroom discussions, and my friends and I could never agree on the most likely scenario. When the subject of the Stooges came up, two of my classmates always said the same thing. Judy Fuhrman said she was related to Larry. He was her uncle, she claimed, but wasn't sure what had become of him. Over time, her story changed a bit, with her ultimately identifying Larry as her grandmother's cousin. Her grandmother's name was Fran Feinberg. Another friend, David Stein, claimed that his brother and sister had met the Three Stooges in New Jersey, and said he had a picture of the five of them together. However, whenever I visited him and ask to see the picture, he was never able to find it. Other friends insisted that Curly and Shemp were still alive (despite published obituaries), while others suggested that *all* of the Stooges were deceased.

In trying to sort out fact from fiction, I was always on the lookout for clues leading to the whereabouts of the remaining Stooges.

News of Larry

My single biggest clue arrived in early 1973, with receipt of the March 14th edition of the *Philadelphia Evening Bulletin* newspaper. Upon skimming the contents, I was overjoyed to find an article entitled, "Larry Fine's Brother Relates History of 3 Stooges." The article was based on an interview with Morris Feinberg, Larry's brother, who was born and raised in Philadelphia, and still lived there after nearly seventy years. The article contained several key pieces of information previously unknown to Stooge fans. Most importantly, it revealed that seventy-year-old Larry Fine was still alive, although partially paralyzed since suffering a stroke three years earlier. It also mentioned that he was living at "The Motion Picture Retirement Home" in Los Angeles, California. According to the article, Moe Howard was also alive — and still active in his seventies.

I was interested to read that during Larry's frequent visits to his hometown he indulged himself with Breyer's ice cream and Tastykakes, two products manufactured in Philadelphia. An accompanying photograph of Morris made clear the resemblance to his famous brother.

Armed with information about Larry's current whereabouts, I telephoned the Los Angeles branch of directory assistance and asked if they could provide the street address of The Motion Picture Retirement Home. My goal was to send Larry a letter and request an autograph. The operator said she was not allowed to provide street addresses, only telephone numbers. I apologized for calling and quickly hung up. I then decided to call back and request the telephone number. In doing so, I reached a different operator. She asked if I was referring to The Motion Picture and Television Country House and Hospital, located at 23388 Mulholland Drive in Woodland Hills. I was speechless for a second; the previous operator had made it clear she could not provide a street address — and this operator gave me the address without even asking! I frantically wrote down the information and replied, "Yes, that's the correct address." The operator provided the phone number, which I ignored, because now that I had the address, I no longer needed the phone number.

That evening, I penned a fan letter to Larry and placed it in the mail the following day. In my letter, I requested an autograph and enclosed a self-addressed-stamped envelope.

CONNECTING WITH LARRY

Five days later I was thrilled to find my self-addressed envelope amidst the incoming mail. I was howling with excitement as I explored its contents: a 3" x 5" card personally inscribed by Larry Fine and a small publicity photograph of the Three Stooges from their 1935 short, *Pardon My Scotch*. This too had Larry's inscription.

Wow, I couldn't believe it — *Larry Fine* had responded to *my* letter, and he did it so quickly! That meant he must be in reasonably good health and was receptive to his fans. The gears started turning in my head as I wondered whether fans could visit Larry — and how neat it would be to hear Larry talk about his experiences with the Stooges.

Coincidentally, my dad announced that he was planning a business trip to Los Angeles that April. I asked him if there was any way he could attempt to visit Larry during his trip. He said that he might — if time permitted. I immediately wrote to let Larry know of my dad's intentions. I also purchased every variety of Tastykakes available and packaged them in a shoe box decorated with gold wrapping paper, for presentation to Larry. I also put together a list of about twenty questions for my dad to ask him and borrowed a cassette tape recorder, so my dad could record the answers.

Upon my dad's arrival in Los Angeles, he found directions to Woodland Hills and drove straight to the Motion Picture Country House, in search of Larry. When he stopped at the reception desk and asked to see Larry, it was around ten in the evening. He was informed that visiting hours were over for the day, so he wouldn't be able to see Mr. Fine. My dad said he had brought Larry a gift

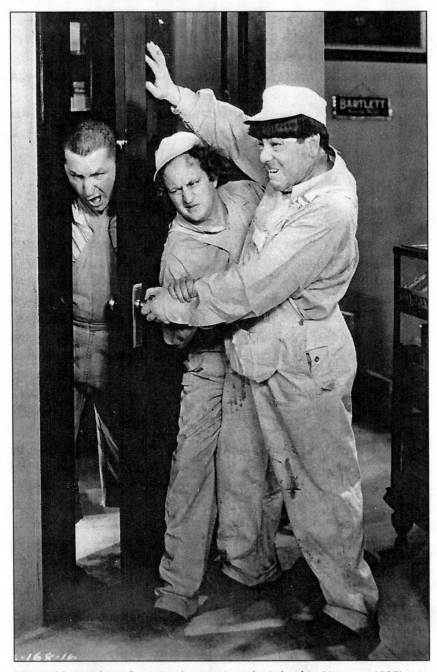

This publicity photo from *Pardon My Scotch* (Columbia Pictures, 1935) was but one of several pictures that Larry Fine sent to his fans.
COURTESY OF SCOTT H. REBOUL

from Philadelphia and that Larry was expecting him. This elicited a discussion of Philadelphia, after which the receptionist agreed to check and see if Larry was awake and open to a visit.

He was. And he told the receptionist he had been looking forward to this visit. So, despite the late hour, my dad was invited in.

Larry was watching a Dodgers game on television when my dad entered the room.

"Hello, Mr. Fine."

"Welcome!" Larry exclaimed as he turned off the television.

Larry was the perfect host. He had no qualms about answering the long list of questions I had prepared or about being recorded. During the interview, Larry provided a substantial amount of information about himself which is now well known, but was news to me at the time. He reminisced about growing up in Philadelphia and talked at length about his many years as a Stooge. He shared his likes and dislikes, such as his favorite television program (*Rowan and Martin's Laugh-In*); his favorite full-length Stooge film (*The Three Stooges Meet Hercules*); and his favorite "Third Stooge" ("Curly — the original Curly — the *best* — absolutely!").

Two of the discussions captured on tape were of particular interest to me. The first had to do with Fran Feinberg, my classmate's grandmother whom — I had been told repeatedly — was related to Larry. When my dad asked Larry about this, the following dialogue transpired.

LARRY: Yes, she happened to be my cousin — my aunt's daughter. And we were practically raised together.

MY DAD: Was that in Philadelphia?

LARRY: Yes, downtown Philadelphia on a street called Mildred Street.

MY DAD: Mildred Street — I don't know where that is.

LARRY: Near Porter and Ritner.

MY DAD: Oh, I know where that is.

LARRY: Well, her parents were raised at Forty-fifth and Spruce.

There it was: First-hand confirmation that my friend's grandmother was *truly* Larry's cousin. And a bit of information on Larry's Philly roots, to boot!

Then there was Larry's bittersweet (yet amusing) reaction to the Tastykakes . . .

LARRY: I got a letter from Scott and he told me about you coming with the Tastykakes.

MY DAD: Do you have any problems eating Tastykakes? Can you eat some of those things?

LARRY: I can eat a little of it — I'm a diabetic.

MY DAD: I see.

LARRY: I cheat once in a while.

MY DAD: Well, we don't want to get you in trouble. Maybe you can give it to your —

LARRY: (interrupting) I can have one!

MY DAD: Okay.

When my dad returned home, he presented me with the tape recording and told me the details of his visit. He described Larry's current appearance and explained how the stroke had affected his mobility. Larry was in a wheelchair, he said, and the left side of his body appeared to be almost totally paralyzed. His hair had turned grey and was now relatively straight and combed back; gone were the frizzy curls he had sported during his long career. But despite these changes, Larry was very upbeat and gregarious — and very much at ease.

My dad's meeting with Larry was everything I had hoped it would be. More than anything, it made me want to meet him. Who would have thought that a world-famous performer would be so accessible to fans? His down-to-earth attitude is perhaps best exemplified by the response he gave when asked if spending his life as a Stooge was enjoyable and fun:

"It wasn't fun; it was work — but it paid off good, so I enjoyed it."

MOE COMES TO NJ

One key piece of information Larry told my dad was that Moe Howard would soon be appearing at a theatre in New Jersey, close to Philadelphia. This was both surprising and exciting, because I just happened to live in New Jersey (near Philadelphia), and I couldn't think of anything I'd rather do than see Moe in person.

I told my friends and neighbors to keep a lookout for any information regarding the date and location of the show. Within about a week, folks started bringing me clippings from local newspapers advertising Moe Howard's appearance at the Walt Whitman Theatre in Pennsauken, New Jersey. Performances were scheduled for Saturday April 28th and Sunday April 29th, with show times at noon, two-o'clock and eight-thirty p.m. The admission price was $1.50, which seemed pretty inexpensive, even back then. As publicized in the advertisement, the event would include a showing of Stooge shorts coupled with Moe's personal recollections.

There was a complication that worried me, however. I was going to be in Germany on a school-sponsored trip the week prior to Moe's show. I was scheduled to arrive back home on the morning of April 29th, the day of the final performances. Having paid in advance for the Germany trip, I was committed to go. As any Stooge fan can imagine, the primary thought going through my mind was whether I'd get back to New Jersey in time to see Moe.

The return flight was delayed, but not so much that it prevented me from being at the Walt Whitman Theatre in time for the Big Event. In fact, I was able to get there an hour in advance, which allowed me to secure a seat in the front row, mere yards from the

Moe on stage at the Walt Whitman Theatre, Pennsauken, New Jersey, in April 1973. This photo, taken by Scott Reboul, later appeared in the 1977 Citadel book, *Moe Howard and the 3 Stooges*, on page 189.
COURTESY OF SCOTT H. REBOUL

stage. I had brought an old rangefinder camera with me and had loaded it with extra high-speed film, in order to capture images of Moe in action.

Shortly after noon, the lights dimmed and a Three Stooges short — *Dizzy Detectives* — appeared on the screen. Although I had seen this film countless times on television, there was something exhilarating about seeing it in a theatre. Part of the excitement had to do with the crowd's spontaneous reaction, which was absent when watching the comedies at home. The other factor had to do with knowing that Moe Howard was *there*, waiting to go on.

The short ended, a spotlight flooded the stage, and Moe made his entrance. Seeing him standing just ten feet from me was a thrill! And to think that just weeks before, the chance of such an event occurring would have seemed completely remote. Yet there he was, looking well and very much the same as he did in the shorts. The most noticeable change was his hair color, which was now white. In truth, his hair had been white for decades, but that had been masked by black hair dye. Hair color notwithstanding, Moe — at the age of seventy-five — looked fit, spoke articulately, and exuded the same impeccable timing he had displayed for so many years on the screen. I naively imagined that there were many more Three Stooges films that could be made. At that moment, it seemed as though there was no end in sight.

After a few introductory remarks, Moe provided a summary of the Stooges' history, starting with their vaudeville days and ending with information on their most recent performances. He mentioned Larry's stroke and said it precluded the possibility of more Stooge films in the future. As Moe spoke of Larry, his voice cracked and his eyes briefly filled with tears. Whether this response was choreographed for dramatic effect or whether it was spontaneous is unknown, but it clearly showed Moe's affection for the "middle" Stooge. Moe then spoke of his brothers, Curly and Shemp, touching on their personalities and confirming the years of their deaths. He also mentioned Joe Besser and Joe DeRita. Besser, he said, was still active as a voiceover artist and DeRita was retired. This was welcome information to me because it left open the possibility of tracking them down and getting in touch with them.

Following the biographical information, Moe left the stage while another short was shown: I believe it was *Husbands Beware*. Moe then returned to the stage, combed his hair down to replicate the classic "Moe look," and began performing some of the vintage Stooge routines. In doing so, Moe played all three roles: himself, Larry, and the Third Stooge. What was amazing about this presentation was that although Moe didn't sound like his partners, he evoked the atmosphere of the old act — and elicited waves of laughter. Clearly, these routines were a part of him and illustrated his great skills as a showman. After taking a few questions from the audience, he left the stage to unanimous cheers and applause.

The show was a delight. It provided me with a clear picture of the Stooges' careers and satisfied my curiosity regarding their current status. It also allowed me the chance to photograph Moe, thereby documenting the experience. When I processed the film, I was pleased to find the photographs were properly exposed and in focus, although expectedly grainy due to the high-speed film. I had 8" x 10" prints made of the best pictures and wondered if there was a way I could get the photos autographed by Moe himself.

The following week, a friend of mine told me he had just received a note from Moe, after writing to him in care of Channel 29 (the station that was broadcasting the Stooges' shorts). The envelope had a return address with a Los Angeles P. O. Box number on it. Using this address, I sent Moe a letter telling him how much I enjoyed his live show and enclosed two copies of the 8" x 10" photo, one for him to autograph and one for him keep. Of course, I enclosed a large self-addressed-stamped envelope to make it easy for Moe to send the photo back to me.

Like Larry, Moe responded quickly. I received the autographed photo and a personal thank you note from Moe within a week. Also enclosed in the envelope was an autographed composite photograph showing four recent publicity shots of Moe, in various poses and attire. To say I was pleased would be an understatement.

Over the coming weeks, I sent Larry and Moe additional letters. I included a copy of the publicity photo that appeared in the *World Book* Encyclopedia under the subject heading of "Comedy." Both Larry and Moe wrote back, providing answers to my questions and asking me follow-up questions, suggesting they both welcomed the correspondence. Clearly, both men were interested in their fans!

A TRIP IS PLANNED

After corresponding with Larry and Moe for a couple of months, I began wondering how I could meet them in person and have my picture taken with them. Coincidentally, my dad was planning another business trip to the west coast in mid-August and I saw this as my chance. He agreed to let me go with him provided I met two conditions:

1) I had to receive word from Larry and Moe that they were amenable to the visits and have specific dates and times for the meetings.

2) I was to pay for my own airline ticket.

After agreeing to these terms, I contacted Larry and Moe by mail, informing them of the proposed dates and asking if and when I could meet them.

Larry's response arrived first:

> "Your letter received and you are welcome any time you come. However, you say you can't come on Aug 9th. That is a Thursday. Friday morning I go to therapy from 9 till 11 in the morning, then I have lunch from 12 to 1 p.m. So you can come any time from 1 o'clock on, on Friday. Saturday morning I rehearse with a wheelchair group till around 11 a.m., then I have lunch till 1 p.m. I usually engage in a Shuffleboard Tournament till 2:30, but if I know you're coming I can skip that. The best thing is for you to call me on the 9th and then we can set a date and time convenient to us both. Of course, every evening would be fine."

A day or two later, Moe's response arrived:

> "I'm awfully sorry but I will be in New York City from August 6th to August 13th — visiting with my son — and on August 14th I believe I will be in Philadelphia to appear on a taped interview with Mike Douglas. Sorry old boy — perhaps some other time."

Although I was disappointed that Moe would be out of town, I was thrilled by Larry's availability and decided that visiting him alone would make the trip worthwhile. Unfortunately, the following week my dad informed me that his business trip had been cancelled, making a visit with Larry impossible. However, things worked out for the best. Through his job at RCA, my dad obtained tickets for Moe's August 14th appearance on *The Mike Douglas Show*. (RCA was the parent company of NBC, which was affiliated with the production of the program.)

TALK SHOW STOOGE

On the afternoon of August 14th, my parents, grandparents, brother and I arrived at the television studio located at Independence Mall (4th and Market Streets) in Philadelphia. We checked in at the front desk and were informed that we could enter the studio early, before the rest of the audience, since our tickets were provided by the station's manager.

Upon entering the studio, I noticed two individuals who were already seated. One of them I recognized immediately — it was Morris Feinberg, Larry's brother, whose picture had appeared in *The Philadelphia Evening Bulletin*. Seated immediately in front of him was a woman I didn't recognize. I approached Feinberg and told him I recognized him from the article. I also told him about my correspondence with Larry. He was very interested and immediately began sharing tidbits about growing up with his famous brother, and of accompanying the Stooges on some of their early stage tours. I remember him saying that one summer in the 1930s, the Stooges were appearing on the Steel Pier in Atlantic City. On that same bill was the comedy team of Bud Abbott and Lou Costello. He said, "It was during these performances that Costello raised the pitch of his voice after hearing how positively the audience responded to Curly." He then took out his wallet and showed me a photograph he carried of himself, posing smugly alongside Larry, Moe and Shemp.

After talking to Morris for several minutes, he asked if I had met Moe Howard's wife, Helen.

It turns out that Helen was the woman who had been sitting directly in front of us, in the front row. I told her I was delighted to meet her and that I was here because of a note Moe had written to me. I explained that I had seen his performance at the Walt Whitman Theatre in April, and had hoped that some day I would get the chance to meet him face to face. Helen beamed as I spoke about her husband and said I could meet him after the taping of the show.

"Just wait at the door in the front of the building — the one facing Market Street," she said. "Moe will be glad to see you."

Shortly thereafter, the doors of the studio opened and the general audience was admitted. Guests appearing on that day's show were then announced: Co-host Soupy Sales, Moe Howard, Lawrence Harvey, W. C. Fields' grandson, and a satirical singing group calling themselves The Creep. Not surprisingly, when Moe's name was announced, the audience went wild.

A clip was shown from the classic 1945 Stooges short *Micro-Phonies*, which brought down the house. After this, Moe made his entrance. He had an instant rapport with the audience, and the audience response didn't let up until Moe left. There was a hilarious sketch featuring Moe, Soupy and Mike in which they recreated the famous "Maharaja" routine — the one featured in the 1946 short *Three Little Pirates*. The sketch concluded with a pie fight, including a surprise ending with Moe approaching a woman in the audience and shoving a cream pie into her face. That woman was Helen Howard, but the audience didn't know it. The response to this seemingly random act of pie throwing was one of amusement — and shock. Most surprising was that Helen Howard was not expecting the pie, so it was as much of a shock to her as it was to the audience. Afterwards, Helen said Moe had never before hit her with a pie — and she was honored it had finally happened.

After the show ended, I raced to the studio exit and waited for the Howards to appear. Ten or fifteen minutes passed. And then, Moe and Helen passed through the doorway, hand in hand. I immediately greeted them, and introduced myself to Moe, shaking his hand. I showed him the letter he had sent me — the letter responding to my request for a meeting in Los Angeles — and he snatched it out of my hand and wrote the following words on the outer envelope:

"Sorry you didn't get to LA to say hello — Sincerely, Moe."

During our conversation, Moe noticed a fan filming us with an 8mm movie camera. Moe automatically transformed himself into his screen persona and began bopping me on the head and acting as if he was poking me in the eyes. Of course, I was thrilled to be a part of his antics. What I wouldn't give to have a copy of that film today!

Unfortunately, I hadn't brought my own camera and had no means of recording our exchange. It is my only regret; all other aspects of the day's events had been perfect. A line of fans waiting to see Moe had formed behind me, so I stepped aside, but not before thanking him for the years of laughter he had given me. I also asked if he would be returning to the area in the near future. Helen said, "Yes, in the next couple of months," although she didn't yet know the exact dates. She advised me to watch for newspaper ads announcing Moe's return.

Although my time with Moe was limited that day, I could tell he was a highly intelligent man, one who was intent on pleasing his fans. When he was in the spotlight, he was gregarious and extroverted. Out of the spotlight, he was serious and soft spoken. He seemed very protective of Helen, and she was obviously very proud of him. They complemented each other perfectly. According to Moe, Helen even wrote some of the Stooges' shorts.

"You know my wife wrote one of the very excellent stories we did called *Hoi Polloi*," Moe told an interviewer. "She used to nudge me in bed, like at two o'clock in the morning, and whisper, 'Honey, I thought of something that would be very funny in one of your scenes.' I said, 'Well, why are we whispering?' And she says, 'I don't want to wake you up!'"

A FAMILIAR FACE

Over the coming months, I corresponded regularly with Larry. In his letters, he often referred to the upcoming publication of his autobiography, *Stroke of Luck*. Several aspects of this book excited me. *Stroke of Luck* would be the first full-length book devoted to the life of a Stooge, and would offer previously unpublished insights into the comedy team. Furthermore, Larry had offered to send me an autographed copy of the book once it was available — which made me doubly excited because I knew the autograph would make the book a collector's item. Lastly, the book would be marketed through a television commercial featuring Larry — which would give fans like myself a chance to see him as he appeared today. Day by day, I waited for an announcement that Larry's book was finally available.

In November 1973, my waiting paid off when I was watching Channel 29's daily showing of Stooges shorts and Larry's commercial appeared on the screen. I was ecstatic to be able to catch this rare glimpse of the retired Stooge. Although the picture and sound quality of the commercial were not too great, just seeing and hearing Larry made it seem as though the Stooges were still in force. Sure, Larry's speech was a little slurred — and he was now in a wheelchair — but there he was, with his familiar porcupine hairdo extending from his scalp and his personality shining through. Just like in the Stooges comedies.

MOE RETURNS

Days later, news of Moe's return to the local theatres started appearing in the newspapers and on Channel 29. This time Moe would be performing at four theatres: the Walt Whitman in Pennsauken, NJ; the Harwan in Mount Ephraim, NJ; the Glen Oaks Cinema in Laurel Springs, NJ ; and the Theatre of the Living Arts in South Philly. One of the dates Moe would be at the Harwan was the same day we had a school holiday, Friday November 15th. I planned to go, of course — and this time I would be sure to bring a camera.

Arriving at the Harwan Theatre on the appointed date, I mentioned to the owner of the theater that I hoped to have my picture taken with Moe.

He thought otherwise: "Absolutely not! No one's going to bother Moe with a *picture.*"

This was disappointing to hear, but I gained new hope when I entered the theatre and spotted Helen Howard seated in the front left section. I approached her, reintroduced myself, and reminded her of our meeting at *The Mike Douglas Show.* She said she remembered me. She also said that she and Moe would be leaving the theatre after the second speech, while the remaining Stooge films were being shown.

Scott and Moe outside the Harwan Theatre in Mount Ephraim, New Jersey, in November 1973. COURTESY OF SCOTT H. REBOUL

"So if you want a photograph with Moe," she suggested, "just follow me as soon as he leaves the stage."

I did exactly as I was instructed. In no time, I was standing between Helen and the owner of the theatre — the same guy who told me that having my picture taken alongside the guest of honor was forbidden. I glanced at the guy and could see that he was irritated by my presence. However, with Helen Howard at my side, I felt pretty confident. Moe finally appeared through the backstage exit door and looked our way.

"Honey," Helen said to Moe, "you need to get your picture taken with Scott."

"Of course I do!" Moe replied.

I presented him with a copy of my school newspaper. It contained an article I had written, "The Three Stooges: 50 Years of Comedy and Success." I explained that the article was based on information he had presented at the Walt Whitman Theatre in April coupled with answers Larry Fine had provided through my dad's visit and through letters. I asked Moe if he would autograph a copy of the article — a copy that Larry had already signed — and of course he obliged.

Moe removed his eyeglasses and combed his hair forward to display his trademark bangs. And then — standing beside me — he posed for a picture. This time I was prepared. A buddy of mine who was adept at photography was behind the lens of my camera, capturing the exchange. The picture turned out beautifully. Seconds after it was taken, Moe and Helen jumped into a car and were gone. Their destination was *The Mike Douglas Show*, where Moe would make a surprise appearance from the studio audience and ask Mike's guest, Richard Lamparski, author of the popular series of *Whatever Became of . . . ?* books:

"Whatever became of *The Three Stooges*?"

FIRST STOOGES BOOK

The following week, my copy of *Stroke of Luck* arrived in the mail. The inscription read:

> *To Scott Reboul*
> *a very patient and loyal fan*
> *Thanks for waiting*
> *Sincerely*
> *Larry Fine*

The book was filled with grammatical errors, but still had a wealth of information to satisfy hungry Stooge fans. What's more, the information was presented from Larry's perspective and provided much insight into his personality — his likes and dislikes, his priorities, and his attitude towards his career and his life. It also contained 130 photographs from his private collection. Until the publication of this book, very few of these pictures had been seen in years.

Over the years, Larry's book has received a considerable amount of criticism due to its amateurish writing style. However, it was a very welcome addition when it was released. The fact that *Stroke of*

Luck was the first complete book on the Three Stooges made it a treasure. It still holds a special place in my heart.

New Visitation Plans

In early 1974 I once again asked my dad if there was any way I could visit Larry. His response was : "How much money do you have?"

I said I had somewhere between $150 and $200.

He said, "If you can find a round-trip ticket to Los Angeles for $150 or less, I'll accompany you and be your chauffeur."

Unfortunately, the cheapest airline ticket I could find was $300. I looked into the possibility of traveling by rail — and that, I was surprised to find — was no less expensive than a flight. So I looked into my other options and realized there was only one form of transportation I could afford: The Bus.

Continental Trailways was offering a package called the Silver Eagle Pass, which provided up to thirty days of continuous travel anywhere in the country for $150.

So a bus it would be.

I then dropped Larry a line, asking if he'd be available for a visit during my Spring Break period.

He wrote back, "By all means, you are more than welcome to visit me," and he suggested I call him when I arrived in Los Angeles. That way, he said, "I'll be sure to stay in my room and wait for you."

My dad and I put together a tentative itinerary for our trip. Spring Break lasted a total of ten days, including the weekends. The first three days would be spent on the bus traveling to Los Angeles and the last three days would be spent traveling back to New Jersey. That left four days in California. Although the primary purpose of the trip was to see Larry, we also wanted to do some sightseeing, including a visit to Disneyland and a trip to Whittier to see a friend. We needed to plan our time wisely — one day for Larry, one day for Disneyland, one day for Whittier. And one day for whatever else came along.

T. Todd Reboul poses by the Silver Eagle bus that transported him and his son on their cross-country journey to visit Larry Fine.
COURTESY OF SCOTT H. REBOUL

GO WEST, YOUNG STOOGE

Three days on a bus didn't sound too bad — and it wasn't — although it did require some lifestyle changes while in transit. We had to sleep upright, there was no bathing facility, there were frequent stops, and we had to be satisfied with the food available at the various terminals. But hey, what did it matter? I was on my way to see Larry.

After seventy-two hours of travel, the bus finally pulled into the Los Angeles bus station. My dad rented a car and we drove straight to the hotel. Once there, I telephoned the Motion Picture Country House to speak with Larry and arrange a time for our meeting. The receptionist said that Larry wasn't there; he had left with family members who were visiting from Philadelphia. I asked when he would return and the receptionist said she didn't know, although she did say that he would probably be occupied with his guests for most of the week. All she could suggest was that I try calling back the following day to see if Larry had returned.

As you can imagine, I was completely unnerved by this news. Could it be that Larry wasn't going to be able to see me? Why, that was the whole point of the trip!

The following morning I called again, hoping that Larry would be there, but bracing to hear that he was still tied up with family obligations. The receptionist answered and said she'd find out if Larry was available. I waited with a knot in my stomach. More than a minute elapsed and there was still no response. Finally, the silence was broken by Larry's simple but warm greeting of "Hello, Scott."

"Hi, Mr. Fine," I shouted, excited to be hearing Larry's voice at last.

"How are you?" he asked.

My response was as innocent as it was embarrassing: "Fine."

What a silly thing to say to someone whose *name* was Fine, I thought. Throughout the remainder of the conversation, I was careful to use alternative words: Good, Great, Wonderful . . . *Anything* but Fine!

Larry asked about my trip and said he'd been looking forward to my visit. He suggested I stop by the following day, which was a Monday. Just then he remembered a schedule conflict and suggested that Tuesday would be more convenient. I was relieved that he had set a date for our meeting, but was a little concerned that another conflict would arise. My concern was unnecessary, as the visit went off without a hitch.

A Memorable Afternoon

My dad and I arrived at The Motion Picture Home right on schedule. Larry was waiting in the reception area of a building known as the Lodge. We could see him through a large front window, waving us in. He greeted us warmly and took us for a quick tour of the facility. The new carpeting, he said, was being installed at a cost of $40,000. The generous benefactor: The King himself — Elvis Presley. We accompanied Larry into his private room, and remained there for the next couple of hours.

Larry was very easy talk to, and spoke openly about a variety of subjects. We discussed his childhood in Philadelphia, his experiences in vaudeville, his life as a Stooge, and his daily activities and

Scott and Larry squint into the California sun in the parking lot of the Motion Picture Country Home, in the spring of 1974.
COURTESY OF SCOTT H. REBOUL

hobbies. We also touched on sports, world affairs, politics, art, music, movies and his fan mail. Larry said he tried to answer every one of the cards and letters he received, but that he was having difficulty keeping up with the constant flow. This was confirmed by the stacks of mail on the floor — there must have been at least 500 letters. Larry showed us many of his favorite photographs, including some of his family members, and some from his days as a Stooge. He also showed us examples of his own original artwork, including a painting of an eagle that he had just completed.

Larry was so personable, and such a great conversationalist, that he made me feel entirely comfortable and never at a loss for words. What's more, he turned the focus on me by asking questions about my schoolwork, hobbies and goals. It made me feel as though I were the most important person in the world! Here I was, visiting with one of the world-renowned Three Stooges, and he was interested in hearing about what made *me* click. And he listened closely, too. I know this because he was able to repeat the information back to each of the residents he introduced me to at the Home. One such resident was Blossom Rock (also known as Marie Blake), who was Jeanette McDonald's sister and an actress herself. She is best remembered for her role as "Grand-ma-ma" in the 1960s television sitcom, *The Addams Family*. Blossom Rock also had a brief supporting role in the 1961 feature film, *Snow White and The Three Stooges*.

Naturally, I asked Larry about his former partners. I knew Curly and Shemp were dead, and that Joe Besser and Joe DeRita were still alive, but I didn't have any hard facts regarding their current whereabouts. And I knew nothing about the status of the Stooges' supporting players, Vernon Dent, Christine McIntire and Emil Sitka. However, I didn't want to take the focus off of Larry and was therefore hesitant to ask detailed questions about those individuals. I decided to address the topic in a general manner.

"Are any of the people from your films still around?"

"Who do you mean?" he asked.

"I was wondering about Vernon Dent, Christine McIntire and Emil Sitka."

"Well, Vernon Dent died about ten years ago — he had diabetes and went blind. I've heard Christine McIntire lives in Los Angeles, but I haven't had a chance to get in touch with her yet. And Emil Sitka — he lives in Los Angeles and is doing fine. He stopped by to see me last week. Why don't you get in touch with him?"

I said I'd love to, but I don't know where he lives.

"His address and number are in the Los Angeles phone book," Larry said, "but I can give you the information." And with that, he pointed to a little address book on his desk and said, "Emil's information is in there, under "S" for Sitka. Help yourself."

As I was copying the number down, Larry seemed to read my mind, as his next statement was, "You're in touch with Joe Besser and Joe DeRita, aren't you?"

Again I said, "I'd love to be, but I don't know where either of them live."

Larry said, "Well, their addresses and phone numbers are in that same book — go ahead and copy it all down. Maybe you can see them before you go home."

And I thought to myself: That's a fantastic idea! Maybe I *could* see them before I go home.

At this point in our visit, Larry suggested we go outside and get some fresh air.

"I like to get a little sun everyday," he said, while pointing out the attractively landscaped grounds. "It keeps me looking healthy." We settled in at Larry's favorite spot and spent the rest of the afternoon talking about health, money and family. He told us how much he wanted to take a trip to his home town of Philadelphia.

"I don't know when I'll be able to go, but I want to get there within the next year," he said. "That way I can see all my family and friends at the same time. And that would include you, if you're interested."

"*Of course* I'd be interested," I replied, thinking to myself what an incredible experience that would be. At the same time, I wondered if Larry could make such a trip, given his paralysis and advancing age. But I could hope. Larry also mentioned he would like to appear on *The Mike Douglas Show* — just as Moe had — if he ever made it to Philadelphia.

After spending four hours with Larry, I knew it was time to go. I hated to say good-bye. We shook hands, wished each other well, and Larry told me to be sure and stop by for a visit the next time I was in the area. I hoped I'd get the chance to see him again (either in Woodland Hills or in Philadelphia), but I realized his health was an issue and it could be several years before my next trip to California. However, regardless of what happened in the future, I had been lucky enough to spend an entire afternoon with the one and only Larry Fine.

The Search Continues

Our first stop the next morning was 643 1/2 Berendo Street in Camarillo. This was the residence of Stooge supporting player Emil Sitka. Although I didn't realize it at the time, Sitka's house was located just down the street from the building used as the Los Arms Hospital in the 1934 Academy Award-nominated Stooge short, *Men In Black*. Sitka's tiny house occupied the top half of a two-story bungalow, which explained why the street number ended in 1/2. I walked up the stairs leading to the front entrance and knocked on the door. No answer. What's more, no car was in the driveway. I knocked again, but soon realized it was a lost cause. As I walked down the stairs, I saw a neighbor watering his lawn. The man looked up at me, pointed to Sitka's door and said, "He's at work. He won't be home until later."

"Okay — thanks," I said and walked back to our car. I was surprised to hear Sitka was at *work*, because I had assumed he was at least seventy or eighty years old, considering the elderly characters he often played in the shorts. Little did I realize that he had been a relatively young man when he was in the Stooges comedies. At the time of my visit, Sitka was not quite sixty years old.

Home Improvement — Besser Style

The next stop was Joe Besser's residence, located at 5103 Biloxi Drive in North Hollywood. It was a one-story ranch house that was modest yet attractive. I rang the doorbell and didn't have to wait long before a woman answered the door. This, it turns out, was Besser's wife. I told her that I was visiting from Philadelphia and hoping to meet Mr. Besser. She immediately disappeared into the house calling, "Joe-eeeey, there's someone at the door who wants to see you."

Seconds later, Joe Besser was standing in front of me.

"What can I do for you?" he asked pleasantly.

I told him I was a big fan of his and just wanted to meet him. A smile spread across his face as he said, "Well, isn't that kind of you? Let me come outside — I'd invite you in, but I'm having my house renovated and it's a *mess*."

I told him I had been visiting with Larry Fine the previous day.

"How *is* Larry?" he asked with concern.

I told him Larry was partially paralyzed, but that he was recovering and in excellent spirits.

Besser said, "I'm glad to hear he's doing better." He then paused and said, "You know, everyone asks me about my being one of the Three Stooges — but I've done a *lot* more things than just that!"

"I know!" I said. "I loved your appearances on *The Jack Benny Program* and as 'Stinky' in *The Abbott and Costello Show*."

The mention of Lou Costello drew a positive response. Joe beamed and said, "Nobody was a sweeter or funnier man than Lou — he was a great comedian and my best friend –Oh, I miss him!" He then shifted gears and said, "You know I traveled across the country with Olsen and Johnson in *Hellzapoppin*."

My dad mentioned that he had seen Olsen and Johnson performing *Hellzapoppin* at the Municipal Auditorium in New Orleans. Joe said he couldn't remember performing there, but did recall appearing at New Orlean's Saenger Theatre. He switched gears again and began to discuss his home renovation project and directed our attention to the brand new stucco finish on the exterior of his house.

"This was just completed yesterday. Montgomery Ward did it for thirty-six hundred dollars."

My dad — an ever-curious scientist — decided to take a closer look at the finish. As he reached out his hand to gently feel the texture, Besser looked over and yelled, "DON'T TOUCH I-I-I-I-T!"

The inflection and tone were instantly recognizable as those Besser had used for decades on stage, radio, and in movies and television — only now I was hearing them in person in his front yard! At that moment, it became clear that Joe's offscreen persona was not a complete "put on." All I can say is that I experienced an unusual thrill hearing Besser inflict his trademark whine on my father.

Getting to see and hear Besser in person was a delight. He was certainly very friendly, open and amusing — and was obviously

Joe and Scott pose for "just one more shot" in the front yard of Besser's North Hollywood residence. COURTESY OF SCOTT H. REBOUL

pleased to be visited by his fans. When asked if he'd mind being photographed, he replied, "Not at all — you go ahead and take as many pictures as you like." And after each photo was taken, he'd say, "Why don't you take one more, just to make sure you get a good one?"

His attitude couldn't have been more accommodating, especially considering we had just shown up unannounced and had interrupted his day. As we left, he invited us to stop by again the next time we were in the area. We promised to do so.

"By then, my renovation will be done and I'll invite you inside," Besser said. "See you then!"

CURLY-JOE — IN THE FLESH

Not far from Joe Besser lived the sixth and final Stooge — Joe DeRita, known as Curly-Joe. The house — located at 10611 Moorpark Avenue in North Hollywood — was a small, weathered, one-story structure, surrounded by a chain link fence. The entrance gate was adorned with a number of signs:

NO SOLICITORS

NO AGENTS

NO TRESPASSING

BEWARE OF DOGS

My dad took one look at these warnings and said to me, "For this one you're on your own."

So I unlatched the gate and cautiously made my way to the front door. My knock was immediately answered by the sound of barking. More accurately, it should be described as *yapping*. There must have been several small dogs inside that house, I thought. With all that racket, I was sure someone would come to the door shortly, unless of course no one was at home. Time passed. The dogs continued to bark and still no one came to the door. I glanced at the driveway, saw a car, and surmised that someone *must* be there. So I knocked again. This exacerbated the dogs and raised the pitch and tempo of their barks. I waited, but there was still no answer and no evidence of human activity within. I knocked one last time, which riled the dogs to a level that could not be ignored.

And then it happened. Amidst the barking, I detected a low frequency rumbling coming from inside the house. This was exactly the type of sound one would expect if someone of Joe DeRita's dimensions were to hobble to the door.

The door opened about three inches and I heard the words, "What do you want?" directed at me.

Although I had an obscured view of the figure behind the door,

I could see part of a chubby face staring at me — and it wasn't a particularly happy face. But it was clear that I was looking directly into the eyes and nose of Joe DeRita.

He asked again, this time a little louder, "What do you *want*!"

I found my voice, told him I was a big fan of the Three Stooges, and was honored to meet him. I also told him I had spent the previous afternoon with Larry Fine, after traveling from Philadelphia to see him, and Larry had suggested I stop by. My statements didn't seem to impress DeRita, but they didn't exactly agitate him either. That was a positive sign.

"I was snoozing," he said.

I could think of nothing to say in response.

He then said, "Let me get you a picture." Telling the barking dogs to calm down — they had been carrying on during most of our exchange — he left. When he returned, he opened the front door fully, and handed me a color publicity shot from *The Three Stooges Go Around the World in a Daze* and an autographed 3" x 5" card.

I now had a clear view of Joe DeRita, from head to toe. And he was wearing nothing more than a pair of underpants — boxer shorts to be precise — no shirt, no shoes, and no official pants. I can honestly say that seeing someone with Curly-Joe's physique, in the absence of street clothing, is unnerving. Of course, I didn't want to appear alarmed, as I was the one who woke him up in the first place.

Although I had wanted to come away from the meeting with a photograph of the two of us, I couldn't bring myself to ask him for such a favor. With his protruding bare belly and white underpants in front of me, I doubted he would agree to be photographed.

I apologized for waking him up, thanked him for the picture, and left.

Walking away from the house, I wondered if I'd ever have another opportunity to meet Joe DeRita in the future under conditions more conducive to picture taking. I didn't know the answer, but one thing was certain: I could still hear those dogs barking as I stepped into the car.

ANOTHER LA TRIP

Four years passed; it was the summer of 1978. Moe and Larry were now gone. I found myself back in Los Angeles, only this time I was there for an entirely different purpose than my first trip. I decided to again drop in unannounced on "the Joes." Neither had moved from their respective houses.

As before, I stopped at Joe Besser's house first, and found him to be as receptive as he was during my previous visit. This time he spoke of having just had his teeth extracted and of experiencing immediate relief from that procedure. Apparently, he had been having problems with his teeth for some time.

"Oh, my mouth feels so much better now!" he exclaimed.

I didn't stay long, but managed to have a couple of new pictures taken with him. As during the first visit, he was very generous about posing and was insistent that I take enough to get "a good shot."

Then it was on to Joe DeRita's house — although this time I arrived late enough in the afternoon to avoid interrupting his sleep. As before, my knocking at the front door triggered uncontrollable barking from the dogs. However, this time Joe answered the door quickly. I was relieved to see that he was wide awake and fully clothed. His reaction to me was a neutral one, but he warmed up after just a few minutes. He then stepped out onto his porch, took a seat, and spent about an hour talking with me. What he had to say was quite interesting. He recalled many anecdotes from his days with the Three Stooges and spoke with an unmistakable sense of ownership of the team.

By the time I left, DeRita was in particularly good humor. This was fortunate, because it left me with a favorable impression of him, one that clearly would have been lacking if I had stopped after my initial visit. What's more, he autographed several pieces of his junk mail for me (that was his idea), and willingly posed by my side for a series of photographs. When I got home, I was amused to see that he had misspelled the word "friend" in each of his inscriptions — they all read, "To my *fried* Scott, Curly-Joe 1978." Whether this was intentional or not, I will never know for certain. But after listening to the former burlesque comic crack

Curly-Joe and Scott at DeRita's North Hollywood home, in the summer of 1978. Courtesy of Scott H. Reboul

jokes for the better part of an hour, the possibility of the misspelling being intentional seems believable.

Joe DeRita made it clear to interviewers that he found nothing particularly funny about the Three Stooges' brand of comedy. Perhaps this response was the result of hearing fans constantly comparing him unfavorably with the original Curly, a comic genius who was arguably everyone's favorite Third Stooge. Regardless, DeRita played the third Stooge role for more than a decade and was an integral part of the team's revival that occurred after production of the shorts had ceased. That, if for no other reason, makes his place in Stooge history significant.

A MISSED OPPORTUNITY

Regrettably, I was never able to meet Emil Sitka in person. I believe this was just a matter of bad luck, as every time I made a trip to Southern California, Emil was either tied up with work or out of town. And by the time he retired, I was no longer traveling to the west coast. Regardless, between the years of 1974 and 1996, I maintained a steady correspondence with him through letters and telephone calls. Emil was very easy to keep in touch with, because he'd respond to every letter he'd receive and wrote at least one question in every response.

Speaking with Emil on the telephone was a real pleasure. He was consistently enthusiastic, upbeat and funny. He often recited dialogue — and always in character — from the shorts. A typical example of a conversation with Emil came in the closing moments of a 1984 telephone call. We had been discussing his recent trip to Detroit, where he had filmed a cameo appearance in a new motion picture entitled *The XYZ Murders* (ultimately renamed *Crime Wave*). I offer this final exchange from that call as an illustration of his playfulness and vitality. (Bear in mind that Emil was about seventy years old at the time.)

SCOTT: Everyone I know who's a Stooges fan always asks "Whatever happened to Emil Sitka?"

EMIL: Well, tell them he's very much alive! I swim — I'm going swimming right now — I dance, I bicycle, I play paddle tennis, and I have 'eh . . . 'eh, several girlfriends.

SCOTT AND EMIL: (Both chuckling).

SCOTT: That's great to hear.

EMIL: And tell 'em all — like I always say when some of these guys want to hear me on the telephone — "Hold hands, you lovebirds" (delivered in the same voice Emil used when he played the justice of the peace in the 1947 two-reeler, *Brideless Groom*).

Emil Sitka co-starred with the Stooges in every one of their incarnations —
from Curly to Curly-Joe. He was even briefly considered as a replacement
for Larry Fine in the mid-1970s. Sitka is best remembered as the befuddled
minister in the Shemp short, *Brideless Groom* (Columbia Pictures, 1947).
COURTESY OF C3 ENTERTAINMENT, INC.

SCOTT: (Laughing)

EMIL: Well Scott, I'm thankful that you called me — and be sure to drop me a line.

SCOTT: Okay, I'll do that. Thank you very much.

EMIL: Have fun now!

SCOTT: Will do.

EMIL: Alright — bye, bye.

SCOTT: Bye, bye.

Christmas 1996: Emil Sitka (far right) with his son Saxon, daughter-in-law Dorine, and grandson André. This was the last Christmas Emil celebrated, as he suffered a stroke in June 1997 and never regained consciousness.
COURTESY OF SCOTT H. REBOUL

I'd like to share one final thought about Emil Sitka. He loved exchanging Christmas cards, and each Holiday Season, his card would be the first I'd receive. In fact, it was not unusual to find his greeting in my mailbox the day after Thanksgiving. This was something I looked forward to every year — because it meant that Emil was doing well. It also became my official notification that the Yuletide season had begun. In the years since Emil's death, I look back on those cards with fondness and can't help but feel the void created by their absence.

A DOCTOR IN THE HOUSE

The concept of "Stooges Among Us" has proven itself in a number of ways. One example can be found in a note written by Larry to my maternal grandfather, Dr. L. M. Hoffman, who was a physician in Williamsport, Pennsylvania. The letter was written in response to a note penned by my grandfather — a note in which he thanked Larry for many years of entertainment and for taking the time to correspond with me. It reads, in part:

> "Here is something that might interest you. Back in 1923 I played in Williamsport at one of your theatres, which I can't remember the name, and during the act, I accidentally broke my big toe on my right foot. I don't remember the Doctor's name, but I *think* he was the only Doctor in town. Anyway, he set my toe, and I finished the engagement."

What struck me about this is that my grandfather had been a practicing physician in Williamsport since 1921, and might very well have been the doctor who attended to Larry. I asked my grandfather if he had really been the only physician in Williamsport in 1923 and he said yes, he believed so. But he doubted that it had been he who examined Larry.

"I think I would remember if I had worked on one of the Three Stooges," he said.

"But Grandpa," I responded, "Larry *wasn't* one of the Three Stooges until several years later — so how would you have known who he was?"

"Well, I think I would have remembered him, that's all," he insisted.

Although I can never be one-hundred-percent sure that it was my grandfather who treated Larry that day, I have to believe he's the most likely candidate.

Wouldn't you?

UNEARTHING A RELIC

At the start of this narrative, I mentioned my childhood friend, David Stein. He was the one who consistently claimed to have a photograph of his brother and sister taken with the Three Stooges. Over time, I began to question the validity of that claim because he was never able to show me the photograph when I'd visit him. In June of 1975 (shortly after Moe Howard and Larry Fine passed away), David and I graduated from the same high school. Just prior to the commencement ceremony, he handed me a package. I opened it and, lo and behold, it contained an 8"x10" black-and-white print of the photograph I'd been hearing about for years. Yes, this was the picture of his brother and sister, Albert and Franny, standing alongside Moe, Larry and Curly-Joe. And the picture was wonderful — very detailed and clear — far better than I imagined! It turns out that the photograph was taken following one of the Stooges' personal appearances of the early sixties. The location of the photograph was the backstage area of the Latin Casino, a relatively famous nightclub in Cherry Hill, New Jersey, just across the river from Philadelphia. Seeing this photo was very satisfying. It provided one more confirmation of the team's accessibility and omnipresence — and it somehow brought closure to my "search."

Franny and Albert Stein pose with the Stooges after their show at the Latin Casino, Cherry Hill, New Jersey, circa 1960. COURTESY OF DAVID STEIN

LOOKING BACK

After almost thirty-five years, I look back on my brush with the Stooges as being an amazing experience that was a highlight of my high school years. How is it that in an age when personal information was not widely available, nor easily accessed, I was lucky enough to be able to track down and meet these world-acclaimed comedy celebrities? And how is it that the chain of events which led to this worked out so perfectly? Was it just "dumb luck"? Was it a matter of "being in the right place at the right time"? Was it my great desire to connect with the Stooges? Or was it something else? I don't know

Scott Reboul and his dad with Stooge Fan Club president Gary Lassin at the entrance of the Stoogeum, Spring House, Pennsylvania, in October 2007.
COURTESY OF SCOTT H. REBOUL

for sure, but one thing is certain: Throughout their careers, the Three Stooges performed nearly everywhere and befriended fans in every location. What's more, they made a consistent effort to form new relationships at every possible opportunity. This no doubt played a role in their acceptance and popularity. Regardless, I'm thankful I had the opportunity to take part in this experience — an experience that seems more and more amazing with each passing year.

SCOTT H. REBOUL IS A RADIOCHEMIST AT THE SAVANNAH RIVER SITE, WHERE HIS WORK FOCUSES ON THE SAFE DISPOSAL OF RADIOACTIVE WASTE PRODUCED DURING THE COLD WAR. HE HOLDS PH.D. AND M.S. DEGREES IN NUCLEAR ENVIRONMENTAL ENGINEERING AND AN UNDERGRADUATE DEGREE IN CHEMISTRY AND PHYSICS. SCOTT RESIDES IN AIKEN, SOUTH CAROLINA WITH HIS WIFE, DEBBI, AND THEIR TWO SONS, TODD AND MARK. SCOTT'S FATHER, T. TODD REBOUL, IS IN HIS EIGHTIES AND RETIRED. MR. REBOUL WAS INSTRUMENTAL IN HIS SON'S QUEST TO MEET SURVIVING MEMBERS OF THE THREE STOOGES, A FACT THAT SCOTT IS QUICK TO POINT OUT. "MY FATHER HAS UNFLAGGINGLY SUPPORTED ALL MY ENDEAVORS — SEARCHING OUT THE STOOGES IS JUST ONE EXAMPLE — AND FOR THAT I AM GRATEFUL."

BOUNDLESS LOVE
BY JOAN HOWARD MAURER

I remember sitting on the floor in my father's little den. We were working together on compiling material for his autobiography. My mother was encouraging us; she wanted so badly for Moe to tell his life story for the benefit of his millions of fans.

What my mother and I both knew at the time was that Moe was very ill. He had recently been diagnosed with lung cancer. I suppose I knew he was dying but I didn't want to admit it. Instead, I threw myself into the task of helping him with his book. Spread out on the floor before me were images of Moe at every phase of his life — in vaudeville with his brothers Shemp and Curly . . . in movies . . . on television. There were photos of the Stooges standing alongside an endless array of show business luminaries over a fifty year span of time. Some of the individuals were well known to me; some were not. I was writing the captions for these photos and frequently I would ask Moe to help me identify someone. His voice was weak but his retention was wonderful. He instantly recalled the name and even offered anecdotes about that individual. Many of these memories appeared in *Moe Howard and the 3 Stooges*, the book that my husband Norman Maurer and I helped to complete.

Throughout his adult life, Moe had been a constant smoker. He tried to quit, but it was an endless struggle. He referred to it as his "battle with the butts." It finally caught up to him and his health began to fail. As was typical of his caring nature, Moe wasn't worried about himself, only me. On April 2nd, my birthday, and one month before he died, he enclosed a little card in with my birthday present, which read:

A Howard Family Memory, circa 1960: Joan presents a cake to her father
on the occasion of his birthday. Moe's son-in-law Norman Maurer helps him
blow out the candles, as does his wife Helen and his grandson Michael;
Los Angeles, California, circa 1960. COURTESY OF JOAN HOWARD MAURER

> *"Happy Birthday Darling,*
> *— my love for you knows no bounds. Take care of yourself.*
> *Get check ups as often as possible."*

Rereading his card, I came to the realization that there was an
underlying reason for his telling me to have checkups. Besides his
penchant for worrying about me, there was the ugly fact that his
personal doctor had neglected to prescribe chest X-rays for Moe's
yearly checkup that year. If his cancer had been diagnosed earlier he
might have had a fighting chance — but on May 4, 1975, Moe
Howard died of lung cancer.

His "battle with the butts" was finally over.

JOAN HOWARD MAURER HAS SAID THAT, CONTRARY TO POPULAR BELIEF, HER EXISTENCE AS MOE HOWARD'S DAUGHTER WAS A NORMAL ONE: "MOE WAS A LOVING FAMILY MAN. FORTUNATELY FOR ME, HE VENTED ALL OF HIS ANGER ON LARRY, SHEMP AND CURLY." JOAN APPEARED BRIEFLY WITH HER FATHER AND UNCLE IN THE 1935 THREE STOOGES SHORT, *POP GOES THE EASEL*. IN 1947 SHE MARRIED CARTOONIST NORMAN MAURER; THEY HAD TWO SONS, MICHAEL AND JEFFREY. JOAN IS CURRENTLY WRITING A MEMOIR, "STOOGE KIDS," WITH HER BROTHER, PAUL.

MEMORIES OF JOE, MOE AND LARRY

BY JOHN CAWLEY

One of the perks of living in Southern California is getting the chance to see celebrities. A greater joy is the opportunity to know them.

Take Joe Besser, for example. Joe is best known for his time as one of the Three Stooges (1956-58) or as Stinky the Kid on *The Abbott and Costello Show* (1952). His most famous catch phrases were "Not so f-a-a-a-a-s-t!" and "You crazy, you!" However, his career lasted for decades in vaudeville, on Broadway, and in film, television and animation. I first met Joe in the mid-1970s through my friends Greg and Jeff Lenburg, two writers who wanted to meet the Three Stooges. As it turned out, I had the car in the group, so I was drafted to help out. They always said I was lucky I had a car. I agree.

AT HOME WITH JOE

Our first visit with Joe Besser was for an actual interview. He and his wife Ernie lived in one of those quaint tiny houses that make up North Hollywood. Joe answered our questions freely. We then showed him some of our collectibles, including a lobby card for his 1944 feature, *Hey, Rookie!* I gave him the card as a gift, and although he had plenty of souvenirs of his career, he was pleased to have it.

The interview was a success. My notes became a key source for an article I wrote for the nostalgia magazine, *Remember When*.

John presents Joe with an original one-sheet from the 1950 Columbia Pictures short, *Dizzy Yardbird*; North Hollywood, California, 1974.

We were soon visiting Joe regularly, once every two to three months. He became almost a surrogate grandfather to us. Before long, Joe began to refer to us as "his boys." One Christmas he gave us bottles of aftershave. And on one visit he was kind enough to loan us his 16mm print of *Hey, Rookie!* This was in the days before video, when most television stations were phasing out black-and-white programming. So it was a special treat to see the film, and an honor that he shared it with us.

We became regulars at the Besser home during the holidays. Conversation centered on current events; only rarely was there mention of Joe's career. This usually occurred because a phrase or a word would spark his memory.

One individual who stood out in his reminiscences was Lou Costello. Joe spoke of how he had met Lou when they were both very young. According to Joe, Lou had borrowed some his "fussy" persona and gags for his own. Oddly enough, this was never a sticking point for Joe: He spoke fondly of Lou at every opportunity. Even after a book (*Bud and Lou* by Bob Thomas) depicted Costello as a demanding, petty, angry person, Joe remembered only his good traits. Joe loved working with Lou and counted his time on *The Abbott and Costello Show* among the most pleasant experiences of his long career.

He had far less favorable opinions of Milton Berle and Jerry Lewis. Both comedians — in Joe's mind — were egotistical to the point of cruelty.

Berle, he felt, was a great comic. Joe had performed on many of Berle's popular radio shows in the 1940s and remembered how well they worked together. Yet Joe's most oft-repeated tale was of a time in the 1960s when he approached his old co-star on the street. Berle didn't recognize him. Joe was later told that Milton usually went without eyeglasses in public and may not have seen him clearly. But Joe was unconvinced; he felt that he and Berle were so close that he shouldn't have needed glasses to know who he was. During later (more successful) reunions, Joe never mentioned the slight, but it was one he never really forgave. (I was surprised years later when I saw that Berle had provided the foreword for Joe's autobiography, *Not Just a Stooge*.)

Jerry Lewis figured heavily into a similar tale of unforgiven pasts. Joe had been in the cast of Lewis's 1961 feature, *The Errand Boy*. He told of the scenes he had in the film, all of which were tremendously funny.

"By the time we were done shooting the scene," Joe recalled, "the entire crew was laughing."

It was after one such take that Joe talked with a production assistant who had been with Jerry Lewis for years. He told Joe that the scene had been funny — too funny. The assistant then explained that on a Lewis film, any scene in which someone got bigger laughs than the star automatically ended up on the cutting room floor. Joe told us that he hadn't believed this until he saw the finished film.

"Almost all of my scenes were cut," recalled Joe. "When I ran into Jerry, he told me they were cut because of time." But, Joe thought otherwise; the picture only had a 95-minute running time. He knew the real reason.

Joe also became angry when he spoke of the animation producers who utilized sound-alikes (like the actor voicing the Besser-like elephant in the Warner Bros. cartoons). As he put it, actors who did that "were taking money out of my mouth." He also complained that his contract with *The Joey Bishop Show* kept him from appearing in Stanley Kramer's blockbuster 1963 hit, *It's a Mad, Mad, Mad, Mad World*. He said that he was to have been one of the gas station attendants who do battle with Jonathan Winters. (These roles were ultimately filled by Marvin Kaplan and Arnold Stang.)

Joe did have a *few* positive stories about his career. He said that some jobs were surprisingly lucrative. His biggest had been a sixty-second television commercial for Off mosquito repellant in 1968. The commercial ran for several years, and each time it did he received a check.

Though Joe felt he did not always get the historical respect he might have deserved, he was pleased that with the work he did he had gained so many fans. He was always amazed to get letters quoting radio shows gags or dialogue from a guest spot he did on a long-forgotten sitcom. Joe would state that some of the letter writers "remember my life better than I do!"

As I heard more and more tales from him, I began to get the impression that he felt a bit neglected by Hollywood. He told of how some folks who had "come up with him" pretty much ignored him. In truth, Joe never really cultivated friendships among his peers (Lou Costello was the exception). He simply put in a full day's hard work and then headed home to Ernie. I've seldom seen a man so devoted to his wife. It seemed that during every visit, Joe would pull us aside and fill us in on Ernie's medical issues. He constantly feared for her frail health. And Ernie cared equally for Joe. She often said jokingly that she didn't know what he would do without her.

Since the Lenburgs and I had ties to the animation industry, we began playing him up to casting producers, and before long he was working for Hanna-Barbera (voicing the character "Babu" in the Saturday morning cartoon show, *Jeannie*). After several gigs he told us he fired his agent.

"I told him 'my boys' get me more work than you do!" Joe said.

As the seventies ended, so did my visits. My work was keeping me busier and busier and the Lenburgs were moving onto other interests. But my thoughts often turned to Joe and Ernie. One day in 1985, finding myself in need of some information, I called Joe. When he answered the phone, I said, "You may not remember me, Joe, but this is John . . ."

He stopped me cold with, "Of course I remember you! How could I forget John Cawley, YOUU CRAAAAZZY! You're one of my boys!"

Joe died only a few years later, in 1988. It didn't surprise me to hear that Ernie died a few months later. They weren't meant to be apart for long.

STRONG WORDS FROM MOE

Moe Howard was definitely "strictly business" when it came to the Stooges. This came as no surprise since he had pretty much managed the team since the time they broke with Ted Healy. Moe had also invested heavily in real estate through the years. He was rumored to have owned much of Ventura Boulevard — a now-pricey area.

But Moe was also a raconteur. He enjoyed talking about the "old days" and his show business contemporaries. And he was always ready to defend the Stooges against the allegations that they were "too violent." At times Moe reminded me of Lou Costello; that is, someone else who wanted to be respected as more than just a B-comic.

Perhaps my most vivid memory of Moe came from a compliment I attempted to pay him during a visit to his home with the Lenburgs. We had just seen the Super 8mm sound release of *Kook's Tour*, an independently made film that marked the last appearance of the Three Stooges. (It was during the filming of this project that Larry suffered the stroke that confined him to a wheelchair.)

I told Moe I enjoyed the film.

He instantly became tense and demanded to know how I had seen it. He then announced that it was illegal to have! The Lenburgs and I looked at one another uneasily. I replied that it had been purchased through a home movie outfit and named the company (Niles Films).

Moe paused a moment before uttering an, "Oh, yes." He paused again and began telling us how *Kook's Tour* had come about.

On our drive back to Orange County, Moe's reaction was a major topic of conversation. An even more pressing matter was finding our way home through the narrow and winding roads of the Hollywood Hills. As I made one turn after another, we all agreed that there was no need to worry. None of us, after all, was on a schedule, and it was unlikely the road would end and we'd end up driving off a cliff — in the tradition of a Stooges' film. With perfect timing, I made a turn and had to screech to a halt at an old wooden barrier. The barrier marked the dead end of the road, and overlooked a drop of more than 100 feet!

We sat there for over fifteen minutes, just laughing.

THE MIDDLE MAN

Larry wasn't the bossy Stooge; that was Moe. He wasn't the crazy Stooge; that would be Curly or Shemp. He was the sly Stooge. He was the necessary middle-man who commented on ("What a brain") and complemented ("What he wants is a pair of slick slacks") the action. Just as Zeppo brought realism to the Marx Brothers, Larry did for the Three Stooges, without being a true straight man.

At the time I first met Larry Fine, he was living in the Lodge section of the Motion Picture Country Home in Woodland Hills. Like my time with Joe Besser and Moe Howard, the visits came about through my friendship with the Lenburgs. We went to the Home's front desk, signed in, and were then led to Larry's private room.

It was easy to like Larry. He was one of the most openly friendly show-biz folks you could meet. He was totally down to earth; there was nothing pretentious about him. After being in his presence for

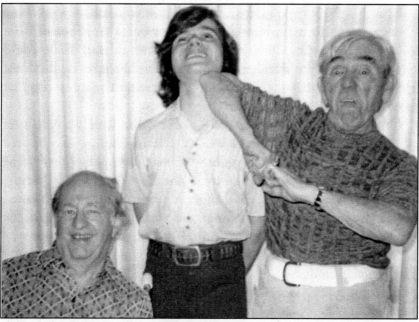

John shyly stands in as the "Third Stooge" in one of the last photos ever taken of Larry and Moe. COURTESY OF JOHN CAWLEY

a bit, you lost all the feelings of being around a "star" or a "sick person." You were just with Larry.

His upbeat attitude was amazing. He would talk of times when money was tight. He would talk of injuries from splinters in cream pie fights. He would talk about deals in which the Stooges never got paid. He talked of the many friends he had lost to death. And never did these tales go in the direction of self-pity or anger. They were simply events in his life, and he had learned to accept them all and move on.

Larry had gotten involved with a book project that eventually went wrong. The book did come out — and was called *Stroke of Luck*. Larry would chuckle when he would tell how some folks thought the title was possibly in poor taste, since Larry was in the hospital due to a stroke. He would reply that his whole life had been a series of lucky strokes. He was lucky to get into show biz, lucky to join the Stooges as it meant steady work, lucky when the shorts ended up on TV because it revived their career. He even felt his stroke had been lucky. For it finally gave him a time to rest and to meet his many fans. And Larry loved his fans.

Though the Home offered fan mail assistance, Larry insisted on answering his mail, himself. He always had a large box of it on a desk in his room. Occasionally a nurse would ask if she could handle some of the simpler ones. Larry would shake his head no. He would state that if the fans took the time to write to him, he would take the time to answer.

Our visits soon became merely social calls. We'd bring 16mm prints of the Stooges' films (as well as other movies), and projected them onto the wall of his room. We also attended some of the Home's social events, such as their annual Wheel Chair Parade. Larry was always up for a good time. He even joined in on a home movie the Lenburgs were making, and actually threw a cream pie we had brought for the occasion! Sometimes we'd just drop by to watch a baseball game with him. Larry was an avid fan of the Los Angeles Dodgers.

On one special occasion, our famous acquaintance traveled to the Lenburgs' high school for a fundraising event. At the conclusion of his talk, the audience went wild, giving him a standing ovation. When the crowd settled down a bit, Larry stated that since they had stood for him, he would stand for *them*. Then, to our complete surprise, he raised himself out of his wheelchair and stood for a few seconds. It was the only time we had ever seen him do it. He said that he had been in therapy for years and wanted to "show off."

It wasn't until one of our later visits that we discovered how much we meant to him. We were sitting around chatting when a family arrived. They had come all the way from Australia to meet him. Larry introduced us to everyone as he signed autographs for the children. When the family left, we told Larry that he should have told us he was having visitors from out of the country. We could, after all, have come on a different day. He looked a bit surprised and said that we were the "important" visitors.

On what seemed like one of our usual visits, we went to check in at the front desk and were told that Larry had a cold and couldn't see us that day. As we left the facility, there was talk of seeing him the following week. I said I wasn't so sure. When asked why, I said that if Larry had simply been sick, he would have either called us to save us the two-hour trip, or had us come in anyway just to say hello. The Lenburgs agreed.

A few days later we heard that Larry had suffered a small stroke, but that he would soon be accepting visitors again.

A week later, he died.

Even though we were still visiting Joe Besser and Moe Howard, I felt a huge loss.

Joe was pleasant and kind.

Moe was polite.

But Larry had become a true friend.

JOHN CAWLEY, A WRITER AND PRODUCER FOR ANIMATION, HAS WORKED AT CARTOON NETWORK, NICKELODEON, FILM ROMAN, WALT DISNEY PRODUCTIONS, WARNER BROS. CLASSICS, DON BLUTH, MARVEL, AMBLIN' AND STARZ. THE CREATOR OF GET ANIMATED!, JOHN IS A NOTED ANIMATION HISTORY AND AUTHOR. HIS OTHER ACTIVITIES INCLUDE PERFORMING PROFESSIONALLY IN COSTUME AND BREEDING GREAT DANES WITH HIS WIFE, RACHEL.

HOW I SPENT MY SUMMER VACATION

BY ERIC LAMOND

Those of us of a certain age will recall many a school year starting with a homework assignment called 'How I Spent My Summer Vacation.' This was an exercise in determining how much we had learned the previous year in English composition classes. These essays were mainly composed of similarly worded stories about similarly uneventful family vacations, trips to visit distant relatives and other mundane activities.

Mine included.

There was, however, one summer that was, for me, very different and very memorable. That would be the summer that I spent working with The Three Stooges.

STUDIO STOOPS

In the mid-1960s, when their popularity was still climbing, The Three Stooges decided to do a cartoon series. These were broadcast beginning in late 1965 and through 1966. Larry, Moe & Curly-Joe filmed 41 "wrap-arounds" — live-action segments which appeared before and after the cartoons. These hurriedly produced pieces were filmed in a Hollywood studio as well as on location at the Balboa Bay Club in Newport Beach, California.

I was fortunate to work on the crew. Did I mention I was in high school? Or that I did not yet have my driver's license? Or that I am Larry Fine's eldest grandchild? No? Well, I was, I didn't and I am. The entire experience gave me lifelong memories which have a surreal quality about them. And I got paid, too!

Eric is inside the suit of armor wearing a hideous monster mask in the closing scene of one of the cartoon series' live "wrap-around" segments.
©IMPERIA ENTERTAINMENT

Imagine getting picked up by your grandfather — who happens to be Larry of The Three Stooges — to go to work. Then imagine being a part of the team with Larry, Moe, Curly-Joe, co-star Emil Sitka, producer Ed Bernds and director Norman Maurer. That was truly surreal.

A lot of work went into each day as the shooting schedule had The Boys working on multiple episodes. So there were scene changes and costume changes and scene blocking and run-throughs and rehearsals and filming — often with several takes.

My duties were many and varied, and changed day by day. I was Larry's stand-in during set ups. I did all that was allowed as a crew member on set construction and equipment moving, as well as all the physical tasks associated with making a film. Because I did not belong to any of the craft unions, there were some limitations on just what I could do.

Since I was a member of the actor unions, SAG and AFTRA, my time in front of the camera was limited as well. If I got too much screen time I would have had to be paid more. So I worked the crew a little, got time on screen with The Boys a little, and thoroughly enjoyed every minute of every day.

One situation called for a monster in a suit of armor to chase Larry, Moe and Curly-Joe. Emil Sitka was lined up to play the part, but the chain mail and armor was a little too small for him. It fit me perfectly, however, so for part of a day I got the star treatment. Now, this is back in the days of Klieg lights, which made for a hot stage and an even hotter monster. During setups for retakes, I was propped up on a big reclining "Broad Board" with electric fans blowing on me and people bringing me water. The production staff teased me, advising me to enjoy it now because when we were done shooting and I was out of the armor, I would once again become just one of the guys schlepping stuff around the set.

When we were done shooting those scenes, Curly-Joe came by and, patting me on the shoulder, said, "Nice work, Eric." He then handed me one of his very large and expensive hand-rolled cigars. I lit it up and enjoyed it for the rest of the day.

Curly-Joe was a lot of fun to be around on the set because he instigated a lot of the fun bits. He would sometimes engage Moe in double talk from the "Maharaja" routine and off they would go with the crew as an attentive, laughing audience. Of course, the director would get frantic because instead of changing out the scenery or attending to the costuming, everyone was enjoying the impromptu show.

The funniest bit they did brought the production day to a standstill. Larry, Moe and Curly-Joe had just finished shooting a scene. We were beginning to set up for another episode when Curly-Joe started singing a rather risqué ditty. Moe and Larry chimed in, and soon they were all singing and dancing. Lyrics were improvised and every prop at hand was used in their dance routine. It was hilarious. During the mayhem they rearranged light stands and scenery pieces to such an extent that we had to pack it in.

One of the lasting impressions of the job was realizing just how hard The Three Stooges worked at their craft. I had been in a few of their feature films and worked with them on some of their television appearances, but that was for just a day or two and limited to certain scenes. Watching them all day long, day after day, week after week caused me to truly appreciate their dedication, professionalism and work ethic. What they produced for us as an audience was pure entertainment magic. How they did it was truly hard work.

At the end of the day, after working with Larry the Stooge, I would go out to the lot and get in the car to be driven home by Larry the grandfather. At home I would be greeted by my mother Phyllis, his daughter, and go into the den and turn on the television to watch my father's TV show: *The Don Lamond Show with The Three Stooges*. So in the course of a half hour I went from working with The Three Stooges on the set to watching their shorts at home. Truly surreal. And every boy's dream.

BLUNDER BOYS

"What was the funniest thing you saw your grandfather do?" you might ask. I'll bet you think it would be something he did in front of the cameras. But it wasn't. The funniest thing I ever saw Larry do was at his house, with Moe and an audience of one — me.

I do not recall exactly how old I was. Larry still had his home in the Los Feliz Hills, as did my folks. So we lived close by and would go visit often. I remember that Moe would frequently be there, and he and Larry would be practicing bits — both new gags and working on routines they had been doing for decades. This day I recall was such a day.

Moe and Larry were working on their trademark slaps and bonks when the phone rang. Larry excused himself and answered the phone. A few minutes later he returned and told Moe he needed some more time to "call back the contractor."

"Contractor? For what?" Moe asked casually.

Larry told him he was having the big bathroom in his den redone. Moe said that he wanted to see it, so he and Larry, with me in tow, went upstairs. Larry explained in detail to Moe what all he was going to have done, which included installing new cabinetry, wall and floor tile, fixtures and hanging new wall paper. This was a very large bathroom, so the work would be extensive.

Art Imitates Life: A classic shot of Moe, Larry and Curly in one of their many decorating disasters, this one from *Tassels in the Air* **(Columbia, 1938).** COURTESY OF C3 ENTERTAINMENT, INC.

Moe told Larry that they could do the work themselves and save Larry a lot of money. Now, please understand that these guys were very handy around the house. When they were not working, they spent their time at home with their families. They were husbands and fathers, in good physical shape, and truly good with tools.

Larry and Moe discussed this for an hour or two, making notes and talking schedules. Larry was convinced that this was a good idea. He told Moe that he would get all the materials and, once everything was delivered, they would coordinate their work and home schedules. They estimated the job would take four, perhaps, five days to complete. They actually wrote out a work plan: one day to remove cabinets and fixtures, one day for wall papering and painting, one day to install the new cabinetry and fixtures, one day for the finish work.

As the saying goes, it looked good on paper.

The big day arrived and, as luck would have it, I was scheduled to spend the day at Larry's house. Larry had actually done all the prep work himself while they had been waiting for the supplies to be delivered. The bathroom had neat stacks of materials and a set of diagrams with work plans.

And so it began. Larry and Moe donned their work clothes: white coveralls, work boots and painter's hats. First on the list was the wallpaper, so two saw horses were set up and topped with big wooden planks. The wallpaper would be carefully rolled out, anchored on each end and covered with glue. More glue would be applied to the walls, and then the wallpaper carefully placed panel by panel, aligning the seams and matching the pattern. That, at least, is the way it should go.

Now, I was sitting on one on the couches in the den and had an excellent view of Larry and Moe starting the process. They rolled out the first panel and began slathering on the glue. In the process, Larry accidentally rolled his brush across Moe's hand. Moe, still looking down, instinctively whapped Larry across the face with his brush. Larry did a typical reaction take, and then whapped Moe with his brush. Moe responded in kind, and soon both Larry and Moe were living a full blown Three Stooges slapstick routine with all the props available — pails of glue, boards, tools, rolls of wallpaper, stacks of tile, cleaning cloths, drop cloths and brushes. They were laughing and having a grand old time.

Me? Well, I was rolling with laughter. These guys were going full tilt, nonstop, through their whole repertoire. They didn't miss a trick, miss a bit or miss a punch, slap, poke, slap or whap. This was Moe and Larry at their slapstick best.

Eventually the routine ended because there was nothing left to destroy. They pretty much damaged everything: the tile, the cabinets, the wallpaper, and the fixtures both old and new. Assorted tools and materials were lying everywhere. They surveyed the mess, shook their heads, tossed their caps and brushes into the heap, joined arms and made a skipping exit out of the bathroom, through the den and down the stairs. From there I am not quite sure where they went because I was still in the den laughing.

Later that day Larry was back on the phone with the contractor.

Later still, my mother, sister and grandmother got home. My grandmother went upstairs and, after a bit, she loudly called out "*Larry . . . !*" My mother decided that would be a good time to leave.

Well, the bathroom finally did get refurbished, and when finished, it looked great.

And it only cost Larry about twice as much.

--- --- --- --- --- --- --- --- --- --- --- --- --- --- --- --- ---

ERIC LAMOND WORKED AS A CHILD ACTOR IN FILMS (WITH THE STOOGES AND OTHER COMEDIANS) AS WELL AS IN TELEVISION (MAINLY COMMERCIALS) UNTIL HIS MIDDLE TEENS. HE RECEIVED JOURNALISM AND ENGLISH DEGREES FROM THE UC SYSTEM AND STUDIED AT THE UNIVERSITY OF VICHY IN FRANCE, AND WAS THE DIRECTOR OF MARKETING FOR C3 ENTERTAINMENT, INC., THE THREE STOOGES BRAND OWNER. ERIC'S THIRTY YEARS OF CORPORATE MARKETING MANAGEMENT IN THE FINANCIAL SERVICES AND HIGH-TECH FIELDS INCLUDE WORKING WITH TRANSAMERICA AND TGI. HE ALSO SERVED AS PRESIDENT OF THE CALIFORNIA HEALTH MAINTENANCE ASSOCIATION'S ADMINISTRATION SUBSIDIARY. ERIC CURRENTLY SITS ON THE BOARD OF DIRECTORS OF C3.

My Six Stooges

by Randy Skretvedt

What little renown I may have comes from my having written a book about Laurel and Hardy. While Stan and Ollie came to be my very favorite comedians, the Three Stooges introduced me to the world of film comedy. I'm grateful to them for that, and I still enjoy them enormously.

My first encounter with the Stooges came in 1963 when I was four years old and saw them on an afternoon children's show broadcast over KTTV, Channel 11, in Los Angeles. The show was *Billy Barty's Big Top*, and it starred the diminutive Mr. Barty — Hollywood's most famous "little person," a comedian himself in movies and onstage from the age of three — as a circus ringleader. He wore a top hat and a swallow-tailed coat, but instead of a three-ring circus, he presided over Three Stooges comedies. (My mother was afraid that I'd emulate the violent behavior of the Stooges, but I laughed so hard at them and obviously enjoyed them so much, she didn't have the heart to make me change the channel. I'm sure she was relieved that I didn't clonk my playmates on the noggin. Well, not often, anyway.)

Every day, Billy Barty would award some lucky boy or girl a brand new Royce Union bicycle. And every once in a while, on a very special occasion, the Stooges themselves would show up to greet Billy and say hello to their young fans. It was Moe, Larry and Curly-Joe, of course; I think I had seen this most recent third Stooge in *Have Rocket, Will Travel*, but otherwise he was new to me. In my four-year-old imagination, I thought the Stooges must be very tall, since they towered over Billy Barty. Later I learned that they were each about 5 foot 4, which I saw for myself when I met them.

By 1965, the Stooges were no longer on the air every day, but Laurel & Hardy were — and although Stan and Ollie became my new favorites, I still tried to keep up with whatever the Stooges were doing. I saw their feature films on television, enjoyed their occasional appearances on variety shows, bought the records they made for Golden, Peter Pan, and Hanna-Barbera, and got the comic books from Gold Key with those great full-color cover photographs.

I didn't see much of the Stooges on TV until about 1970, when we got a new television station in the Los Angeles area. It was KBSC-TV, Channel 52, broadcasting solely in glorious black and white on UHF. At first, the station was on the air only from five o'clock in the afternoon until ten; the first hour was Hal Roach Little Rascals comedies, followed by four hours of travelogues, cleverly titled as new programs: *Flight 52, Travel 52, Adventure 52.* Then there was a five-minute "Meditation" (a sermon by a local clergyman), a film of "The Star-Spangled Banner," and a blast of snow on the screen until five o'clock rolled around again. Before long, though, Channel 52 added new items to its bill of fare, among them reruns of the ghoulish comedy *The Addams Family*, a lesser-known Jay Ward series called *Hoppity Hooper*, two dreadful yet endearing Japanese cartoons (*Speed Racer* and *Kimba, the White Lion*), and — the Three Stooges.

At first, the station ran a solid hour of the Stooges, three complete shorts. Then, some genius decided that it was better to run them in two half-hour slots an hour apart, which meant that instead we'd get four shorts with about five minutes cut from each print (and usually from the beginning of the film, when the plot was being set up). To this day, there are still many Stooge shorts which I don't know very well until the first five minutes have elapsed.

QUESTIONS AND ANSWERS

The Stooges became wildly popular in Los Angeles thanks to the renewed exposure given them by Channel 52. I wondered where Moe, Larry and Curly-Joe were — if they were still alive, planning to make new films. The last new performances of theirs I could remember were on TV variety shows in the mid-1960s, and around that time they'd also made that series of color cartoons with the live-action introductions.

Then, suddenly one day Moe Howard turned up as the guest on a local afternoon show about arts and crafts. He wasn't there to talk about his years as one of the Stooges; he was there to show the ceramics he made as a hobby. (One of them was a sculpture of a puppy, which he used as a tray for his eyeglasses.) It was surprising to see Moe wearing glasses, with a shock of white hair combed neatly back, and it was frustrating that he wasn't telling all sorts of great stories about working with Larry and Curly — but I was glad to see that he was alive and healthy.

In 1973, Moe made an appearance on Channel 52's new show for the teen set, *Headshop*, hosted by Elliot Mintz. The Stooges also got a new sponsor on Channel 52 — Larry Fine, promoting a book he'd written called *Stroke of Luck*. The commercial showed him at the Motion Picture Country Home; he was in a wheelchair, and his slightly thick speech indicated that he'd suffered a stroke, but it was still good to see him — and of course, I put a check in the mail for the book immediately. (For $7.95 plus shipping and handling, as I recall.) The book turned out to be a privately published opus with the byline taken by someone named James Carone; the back cover picture of him, sporting a pompadour hairdo and a suit with wide lapels, was clearly from the late 1940s. The book was distressingly full of grammatical errors and littered with unnecessary commas, but it did have lots of entertaining stories and some great photographs.

Then, I stumbled onto a happy surprise. It was on a local television program over KNBC, Channel 4, called *Sunday*. You can guess what day it aired. The hosts were Kelly Lange and Tom Snyder; within a few years he would be the charismatic host of NBC's *Tomorrow* program and the target of some pointed parodies by Dan Aykroyd on *NBC's Saturday Night*. On this week's program, Kelly and Tom were spending the afternoon at the Country Home and interviewing several of the residents. Among them were character actor Donald Crisp, comedienne Babe London (who appeared with the Stooges in *Scrambled Brains* and with Laurel & Hardy in *Our Wife*), actress Bess Flowers — who was the queen of the extras as well as a memorable foil for the Stooges in *Tassels in the Air* and *A-Plumbing We Will Go*, among other films — and Larry.

In his interview segment, Larry told Tom that he did several speaking engagements every year, often appearing with Babe London. He enjoyed visiting the students at nearby Pierce College and answering their many questions about the Stooges; it was gratifying that new generations of fans kept their work and memory alive.

On March 2, 1974, I got to be one of those lucky fans, and saw Larry in person. It was at Loara High School, in Anaheim, California, just a few miles from my home in Buena Park. Two students named Jeff and Greg Lenburg (fraternal twins who didn't look exactly alike, but who shared the same wacky sense of humor) had become very close friends with Larry. They were active in Loara's drama department and wanted to help raise the money for new curtains and a new sound system for the school theater. Larry agreed to come out and do a personal appearance as a fund-raiser.

The house was packed that Saturday afternoon. Two Loara students, Bill Parsley and Kent Hannibal, entertained the crowd with some ragtime and jazz numbers on piano and drums, and then Jeff introduced the screening of *Scrambled Brains* and *Men in Black*. Even in 16mm prints, it was a treat to see the Stooges on a (moderately) big screen with an enthusiastic audience. And then, with a jazzy piano-and-drum arrangement of "Three Blind Mice," Jeff wheeled Larry onto the Loara stage, to wild applause from the audience. Larry wore a jaunty fedora-style hat and smiled broadly as the crowd cheered him. Despite the slight thickness in his speech, his memory and sense of humor were absolutely intact.

Of the several hundred people who were there that day, I seem to have been the only one who brought a tape recorder. My trusty Sony five-inch reel-to-reel mono recorder worked great in 1974 and still does today, which is why I can now bring you the question-and-answer session from that afternoon. The questions are from all manner of fans, young and old, novices and experts. Jeff occasionally had to repeat the questions for Larry (who called Jeff, "My interpreter!"), but I've edited out those repetitions. The session began with Larry testing his microphone.

LARRY FINE: Can you hear me now? How about this? The reason I'm asking is, I got new teeth just for you folks. And I misunderstood the date — I thought it was May the second, and I thought I'd have time. So when I was at the dentist, I told him to hurry it up and get me a set of teeth. I'm now at the age where I could eat a steak, but I haven't got the teeth anymore. He said to me, "Mister Fine," — he don't know me very well — he said, "You're a brave man." It took him an hour and three quarters to get one tooth out. And he said to me that I'm a brave man. He said, "I've had football players, baseball players, all kinds of athletes, but you're brave." The hell I was! I was paralyzed! And I'm sitting there, I can't get out of the chair. You know, if I could run I would've run the hell out of there! And he's telling me I'm brave. Well, that's the way it goes. I'm here to answer questions. Now, if there's anything you want to know, just shout it out and I'll try to answer it.

Q: Is it true that you really hit each other?

LF: What you see is what we got!

Q: Did you all get along very well?

LF: Off the screen, yes.

Q: Whatever happened to Christine McIntyre, the blonde who was in a lot of the Shemp episodes?

LF: She's around, I guess; I haven't seen her in a long time. But I heard she wrote a biography, a book. I imagine she can tell a few stories! I don't know on who — not on me, I'm sure.

Q: When did you start making films?

LF: Nineteen-thirty was our first film. Shemp was in the first one, then he quit and he went back to New York, and we brought in Curly. Then when Curly got sick, Shemp came back. And that's why everybody thinks Curly was the original, but Shemp was. And after Curly got sick, Shemp came back. And then Shemp died, then Joe Besser came in. Then Joe quit. And in Nineteen-fifty-eight, Joe DeRita came in.

Q: Is Curly still around?

LF: No, he died in Nineteen-fifty-two.

Q: Where are all the old films today?

LF: On TV, I guess!

Q: Is Moe still alive?

LF: Yes, he's still alive. He's seventy-six; I'm seventy-one.

Q: How many films did you make?

LF: Well, we made two hundred of these shorts, one-hundred-fifty-seven cartoons, and twenty-four features. That amounts to somewhere around four hundred and twenty-five.

Q: What about some of your old sidekicks, like Vernon Dent?

LF: They've all passed away. Moe and I have outlived all of them. I guess we're uglier.

Q: What was it like working with Clark Gable in *Dancing Lady*?

LF: Well, it was nice. He was a big star, he demanded a lot of favors, he got 'em. And naturally, working with Joan Crawford and Clark Gable, you get some of the favors, too. But in our shorts, we didn't get that kind of treatment. We didn't even get doubles! We did most of the stunts ourselves.

Q: Where did you get the idea of combing your hair out?

LF: I didn't! That was Moe's idea.

Q: Which one is your favorite film?

LF: *You Nazty Spy* or *I'll Never Heil Again.* Those two where Moe did Hitler. Then for features, I guess it's *The Three Stooges Meet Hercules*, which I think they're going to show today.

Q: Who wrote most of your scripts?

LF: What scripts? No, we did a lot of our own writing. Can't you tell?

Q: Did Moe really control the three of you the way he did on screen?

LF: Nobody controlled us! It was a partnership, pure and simple. Mostly simple.

Q: Is Ted Healy alive?

LF: No, he died in Nineteen thirty-seven. I *told* you we were old!

Q: How did the eye-poking routine get started?

LF: Oh, that started at a bridge game, believe it or not. Moe, Shemp and I played bridge one afternoon. We were working the Paramount Theater, right here in Los

Angeles. And when the last deal was over, I said I had all the honors. And Shemp had just taken a trick with the ace of spades. He said, "You did, eh?" And whack! Right in the eyes! He really did it, knuckle deep. I teared all day. Moe got hysterical. He laughed, and he fell over in the chair, and fell right through a French window, and he cut his hand. And the next day, when we did a gag, he remembered that and poked me in the eye, but he faked it. He never did it really. And I don't advise anybody to do it. Moe knew how to fake it. Of course, you realize that most of the stuff we did was with rubber hammers, fake saws and so on, or I wouldn't be here to tell you about it.

Q: Who gave you the idea to start the Three Stooges?

LF: I don't know. Whoever did, it was a hell of an idea! It lasted for forty-two years.

Q: Are you thinking of making another group, another Three Stooges?

LF: Well, they're talking about making a picture at Twentieth-Century called *The Little Stooges* — they have three young fellows. But I don't know; it'll be according to what kind of punishment they can take.

Q: Are Joe Besser and Joe DeRita still alive?

LF: Yes. Two of them!

Q: Is it true that you have a television series coming up?

LF: No. I'll be lucky enough to get my health back. That's the comeback I'm hoping for. They wrote up in the *National Enquirer* that I'm making a comeback, but I'm going to get my left leg and left arm to come back, and I'll be satisfied with just that.

Q: Where do you live now?

LF: At the Motion Picture Country Home, in Woodland
             Hills.

Q: How much did you make doing the films?

LF: I don't know — it amounts to a hell of a lot of
             dough!

Q: Do you get any residuals from the TV showings of the
             films?

LF: No. We don't get a dime. Thanks to Ronald Reagan.
             He happened to be the president of the Screen Actors
             Guild, and he happened to own part of *Death Valley
             Days* and *General Electric Theater*, and they were made
             in 'fifty-eight and 'fifty-nine. So he compromised,
             and made residuals start after 1960, so he didn't have
             to pay any. And we were through with those pictures
             by Nineteen-fifty-eight. We get 'em for the features,
             but when you don't make a picture for television, the
             residuals are very small. They only count for television
             pictures.

Q: Does Moe live with you at the Country Home?

LF: No, I'm not attractive enough. Moe is married; he'll
             be married fifty years in June. He's got a son, and a
             daughter, and three grandchildren. I have five grand-
             children and one great-grandson. [*Applause*] It was my
             pleasure!

Q: Were you ever hurt badly doing the stunts?

LF: Not real bad, but enough to lay off for a couple of
             weeks. Like a broken arm, or a broken nose, a broken
             toe or ankle, but nothing *serious*.

Q: Do you remember working with Lucille Ball?

LF: Yes. She made one of her first pictures with us, called *Three Little Pigskins*. I thought she was great, and I thought Columbia would keep her. She was only getting seventy-five dollars a week. Think of it — seventy-five dollars. She makes millions now.

Q: Are you and Lucille Ball still friends?

LF: Oh, yeah, sure. She doesn't consider me an enemy. She's very friendly, a wonderful person. She does a lot for actors, too. She doesn't advertise the fact. There are a lot of performers who do that. Jimmy Durante is one, Frank Sinatra — there are a lot of big stars who help the little ones. I wish I was big; I'd help the little guys. I know what it means to the little guys.

Q: How did you do the sound effects on the films?

LF: We didn't. They did it in a lab. And those guys were damn good.

Q: What do you think of motion pictures today?

LF: Well, I can't make them — I don't look good in the nude! No, really, we made pictures for forty years, and never even said a "hell." So you don't have to be dirty to entertain people, I don't think. We proved that you don't. I *think* we did.

Q: What's the story behind your new book?

LF: Well, it's the story of my life, when I started — in life, not in show business. I was hurt when I was a child [here Larry is referring to a childhood accident where he burned his arm with some acid, which caused him to take up the violin as physical therapy]. And it's about the handicaps I had before, and how I joined the Stooges, and the funny things that happened to us. I call it *A Stroke of Luck* because I think it was a lucky stroke that I met the Stooges, and got to be a Stooge. And even *this* stroke was lucky to me, because I got to see other people and realize that no matter how sick you are, somebody else is worse off than you are. And if you stick to it, you're going to make it. Three years ago, they gave me up for dead. They said I'd never walk again, or talk again, and here I am talking, and I'll be walking, you can bet on that! [*Applause*]

Q: You were such big comedy stars at Columbia; why did you only appear in a couple of features there during the 'thirties and 'forties?

LF: Well, mainly because Harry Cohn, who owned Columbia, figured he would rather keep us exclusively in the shorts field — because our shorts were selling better than those damn B-pictures he had. He was making more money with the shorts, so he kept us there. It wasn't until after Harry Cohn died — they'd let us go and had to bring us back, but they figured they'd make features with us instead of shorts.

Q: How did you develop the "Maharaja" routine?

LF: Well, it developed among the three of us. I gave them the idea for "A-ha," I think.

Q: Where did you get the idea for the double-talk, the "Rossbanias Yatchi Benny Footchi," that stuff?

LF: Well, Moe thought of that. Years ago they had a Polish maid who talked that way! And he remembered it.

Q: What kind of job did you have before you joined the Stooges?

LF: My first job was as a violinist with an orchestra. You'll find that in the book if you're ever unfortunate enough to buy the book.

Q: When you were a boy, who was your idol, your show business hero?

LF: Show business? Oh, I don't know. I was a boxer, too, and I was crazy about Jack Dempsey.

Q: Did you ever meet Laurel and Hardy?

LF: Yes, we made a picture with them called *Hollywood Party*. And then I knew Stan when he was sick, after Oliver died. Stan Laurel didn't want to see many people, because he felt he looked sick, and didn't want to see people. I saw him — he had an apartment out in Santa Monica somewhere, on the way to Malibu. But he was a sickly man. And another man who's very sick, who you never hear about, and who doesn't like visitors — do you remember William Powell? He's pretty sick. He's out in Palm Springs.

Q: Were the Three Stooges already slapping each other before you came in? Did the original group start that, or did they start when you joined the group?

LF: No, I don't think they were doing that. They weren't stupid enough.

Q: Where did you get the idea for Curly to start acting strange, for example when he'd hear "Pop Goes the Weasel" and go wild?

LF: Well, nobody — he was wild! He was an original comedian. Anything he did, he originated. And I think there's a few comedians who copied him. Jerry Lewis admitted to me that he copied him, and so did Lou Costello. There were a few others who tried to copy Curly.

Q: Have you ever been to Niagara Falls?*

LF: No, the nearest I got to that was — Moe.

Q: Are you telling us that most of the Three Stooges was basically improvisation?

LF: Well, not everything, but if we started to ad-lib, the director would let it go. He'd say to the cameraman, "Just keep shooting," because always they could cut it out if it wasn't funny. But most of the time, it turned out to be funnier than what was written down. You know, it's like after something happens, you say, "Oh, I should have said so-and-so." Well, that's the way it happened with us — when we started doing the scene, somebody thought of something that would be funnier, and we did it. And it turned out to be funny and we left it in. See, that's the advantage of a movie. You can cut something out or put something back in. You can't do that on the stage.

Q: Who is your all-time favorite comedian?

LF: Oh, I'd have to say Bob Hope.

Q: What was the name of your last movie?

---

* The routine referred to here is in the 1944 short *Gents Without Cents*. Moe and Larry separately recount to Curly a romantic triangle that took place in Niagara Falls — the mere mention of which causes each of them to re-enact the pummeling they gave the other, using Curly as a stand-in.

LF: Well, it's not released. It's called *Kook's Tour*. K-double O-K-S. *Kook's* Tour. We made it up north in Idaho and Oregon and Washington, on the Lewis and Clark trail, on the Salmon River. It's an outdoor picture about hunting and fishing, and what not to do when you go hunting and fishing. And believe me, there's a lot of what not to do!

Q: Why isn't it released yet?

LF: Well, because I got sick in the middle of it, and they're trying to release it without finishing it. But I don't know if there's enough footage. I've only been sick a couple of years. We waited — at first I thought I might be able to go back and work. But now, I'm hoping to just get back and walk and live again. I'm too old to go to work. Or lazy, I don't know which.

Q: Did you consider making the shorts work, or was it fun? Was it a job to you, or was it pleasurable?

LF: It was a way to make money! That's all I could do. After all, when you have a family, you have to bring home the money. My success went to my wife's head. She liked mink coats and diamond rings, trips to Florida, and you don't get those for nothing.

Q: Did the Three Stooges ever make any serious films?

LF: No, I don't think so. The most serious film we ever made was *Snow White and the Three Stooges*. There were a couple of scenes in there which were *sad*. And I don't mean sad, I mean *saaaaaaaaadd!*

Q: Do you ever watch yourself on TV?

LF: Only when I want to punish myself. No, I can't get the cable where I am at the hospital, so I don't get to see it. Maybe it's just as well, because an actor who sees a film he's in don't enjoy it, because he criticizes himself. He doesn't watch the picture as a picture, he watches himself. And believe me, you are harsher on yourself than other people. You know you did wrong — and other people don't know it, but you feel it in your heart. And you know when you don't do something right — it hurts you, because there it is on film. If somebody takes a snapshot of you, and you don't like it, you can throw it away — but you can't throw a movie away. You're stuck.

Q: How long has it been since you've been poked in the eyes?

LF: Three *lovely* years!

With that, there was a large round of applause from the packed house. Greg and Jeff told the crowd that Larry had been driven all the way from Woodland Hills to Anaheim (at least an hour's drive on the Los Angeles freeways, even on a rare good day) to help Loara High School raise money for their drama department. With that, they presented Larry with an award which resembled an Oscar. The audience gave him a standing ovation. Larry then said, "Well, thank you, and just for that, I'm gonna stand, too." He was able to get to his feet, and beamed as the audience applauded. "Thank you all very, very much," Larry said. "This is the closest I'll ever get to an Oscar, so I appreciate it. I'm glad you liked it — I hope you did, anyway. 'Bye!"

Greg and Jeff then wheeled Larry backstage, and while *The Three Stooges Meet Hercules* was being run for most of the crowd, some of us went backstage hoping to thank Larry personally. I was one of the lucky few who got to tell him how much I appreciated his performances — including the great one he'd just given. He signed my copy of *Stroke of Luck* ("Sincerely, Larry Fine 1974") and I could see that despite the stroke he still had lovely hand-writing.

Joe and Ernie

That was my only encounter with Larry, but my first of many with Jeff and Greg Lenburg. Soon afterward, a mutual friend of ours named John Cawley, Jr. brought them to a meeting of the Orange County Tent of Sons of the Desert (the Laurel and Hardy appreciation society), which I was running at the time. John was running a magazine for film collectors; in those long-ago days before the advent of home video, a fanatical few of us spent all of our ready cash on Super 8 and 16mm prints of old movies, mainly comedies. John and the Lenburgs and I were all film collectors, and I began writing for John's magazine, *Private Screenings*.

Our friendship blossomed and the Lenburgs and I remained very close until the early '80s, when Greg moved to Indiana and our lives took different courses. Jeff and Greg and I ultimately went to college together, made lots of zany movies for class assignments, and did research for a number of book projects — in addition to just having a lot of fun. I cherish the memory of those days, and I'll always be grateful to Jeff and Greg, and John Cawley, for inviting me to tag along on their Stooge adventures.

The three of them had become friends with Joe Besser, who lived with his wife Ernie on Biloxi Avenue in North Hollywood. Jeff and Greg had first met Joe in 1972 (and you can read about that in the book the three of them co-wrote, *Once a Stooge, Always a Stooge*). I first met Joe and Ernie around Christmas of 1975, I think. I know it was around Christmas time, because the house was festooned with all manner of bright and shiny decorations — everything was bedecked with ornaments, tinsel and other forms of Yuletide cheer.

I never met anyone who observed Christmas more festively and joyously than Joe and Ernie, which was a little surprising since Joe was raised in an Orthodox Jewish family. Ernie (whose maiden name was Erna Kay Kretschmer) had a variety of European forebears. I remember one time she was trying to recall all the different ethnic groups in her family; she said, "I think there's some French, some Irish, some Jewish . . ." Ernie loved Christmas with an absolute passion and Joe was happy to join her. At other times of the year, their home was pretty colorfully decorated, too — Ernie was a painter, and with her artwork complementing Joe's many

Randy with Ernie and Joe Besser; North Hollywood, California, circa 1975.
COURTESY OF RANDY SKRETVEDT

framed autographed pictures from show-business friends, their walls were mighty interesting.

Joe was pretty rotund when I first met him and was still coloring his hair light brown — so I felt a little dizzy when I first entered the Besser home and shook hands with him. I felt like I was stepping into a TV show, because he looked exactly as he had in Stooge shorts, on the Joey Bishop show, and on a long-running commercial for "Off!" insect repellent.

Ernie was vibrant, energetic, quick-witted — she had a slightly gravelly voice and a perpetual, radiant smile. She was literally colorful, with dark brown hair and bright magenta lipstick. Her personality was like a more bubbly version of Thelma Ritter, with a lovingly sarcastic sense of humor. She had so much energy and vitality it surprised me that Joe had bowed out of the Stooges to take care of her during a spell of ill health.

Joe at first seemed to be annoyed that he was being remembered only for his brief stint with the Stooges. After all, he had worked with Olsen and Johnson, Milton Berle, Jack Benny, Abbott and

Joe and "Wild and Crazy" Ernie pose with their guest's new biography on Steve Martin; North Hollywood, California, 1980. COURTESY OF RANDY SKRETVEDT

Costello, and had been a very prominent second-banana in every entertainment medium. His tenure with the Stooges had only been from January 1956 to December 1957; why, he wondered, was he only being remembered for two years of a fifty-year career?

He had gotten a letter from Emil Sitka not long before; Emil had written about how wonderful it had been to work together at Columbia, and wanted to get together for a joyous reunion. Joe barely remembered Emil and felt a little put out that Emil wanted to be buddies. Joe said, "There are people I worked with for years and haven't seen for a long time, why should I get together with Sitka Whatsis?"

Easing this irritation was the devotion that the Lenburgs showed to Joe and Ernie. Joe always called Jeff and Greg "my boys." They worked tirelessly to promote him to casting agents. He had done quite a bit of voice work for Hanna-Barbera; the Lenburgs hoped to get him more work with that studio, and with Disney, which at that point was still making live-action comedies with many veteran comics in the supporting casts.

In the spring of 1979, Joe had a brief seizure where he was unable to talk for about thirty seconds and one of his arms began flailing wildly; this understandably frightened him and he went to see his doctor, who determined that he had a blockage in his carotid artery. Joe went to the hospital for surgery; part of an artery from a leg was used to replace the blocked section. Greg, Jeff and I went to see him during his hospital stay and I remember him being understandably a bit tired but in good spirits. His doctors had discovered that Joe had diabetes, and put him on a sugar and salt-free diet. Before too long, he'd lost sixty pounds.

As the years went by, Joe let his hair go to its natural white. He also became much more amenable to being remembered for his work with the Stooges. In 1978, Jeff and Greg and I began work on a biography of comedian Steve Martin, who at that point was phenomenally popular. The book was published in 1980, and we brought some of the first copies to Joe and Ernie. Joe was happy to pose with the new authors, and even put on a pair of Steve's trademark bunny ears for one picture.

A Belated Honor

In 1983, a campaign began to get the Stooges a star on the Hollywood Walk of Fame. I'm not sure exactly who instigated the idea. Gary Owens, a very popular radio personality in Los Angeles who was also known nationally for cartoon voice work and for his TV appearances introducing *Rowan & Martin's Laugh-In* "from beautiful downtown Burbank," was very active in the project from the beginning. He was more than happy to promote it on his radio show over "Music of Your Life" station KPRS, located on the 19th floor of the First Interstate building on Sunset Boulevard.

The Lenburgs were, of course, very much involved with the campaign. We got to meet Gary at his KPRS office, and I was delighted to find that he was the nicest person imaginable, the classiest of class acts. I remembered how flattered I was when he got a call, during his on-air shift, from a reporter asking for details about his career; he said to me, "Randy, you know a lot about the different things I've done, could you please talk to this fellow and fill him in?" Fortunately, I did know about *Laugh-In*, Gary's radio work on KFWB and KMPC, his cartoon voices for *Space Ghost* and *Roger Ramjet*, his comedy albums, and many other projects. (Gary also has a phenomenal memory. In 1991 I happened to be at a re-creation of some old-time radio shows produced by alumni of Los Angeles City College. Gary and Steve Allen were the hosts of the event. I hadn't seen Gary since that one time in 1983, but after the program, at a post-show party, he came up to me and said, "Hello, Randy!," recognizing me instantly. I was amazed.)

The campaign to get the Three Stooges a star on the Hollywood Boulevard sidewalk got plenty of publicity, and many flesh-and-blood stars were happy to add their endorsements. Finally, in August 1983 the Stooges were honored with a star and the accompanying ceremony. Milton Berle and a number of luminaries were there, but Joe Besser was the one member of the team in attendance. I remember him saying to the large crowd, "I see four clouds overhead, and do you know who I think they are? It's the boys!" Meaning Moe, Larry, Curly and Shemp. Joe was convinced that they were looking down from their eternal home and sending a message of thanks to their fans.

It was lovely that Joe came to terms with being remembered primarily for his work in the Stooges, and that he was proud to represent the team on the day they were finally applauded by the Hollywood elite. Recognition for the Stooges may have come "not so faaaa-a-a-st!," but when it arrived it was truly heartfelt.

MOVIE MANIACS AND CURLY-JOE

I mentioned that John Cawley, the Lenburgs and I were all collectors of old comedies on Super 8. If we were movie addicts, a wonderful guy named Mike Lefebvre was our genial pusher. He ran a mail order company called L/C Distributors, and was able to get all sorts of great comedies and cartoons for us; I remember how happy we were when Columbia finally decided to release some of the Stooge two-reelers complete in Super 8 sound. Before, we'd had to content ourselves with silent ten-minute cut-downs of a handful of the films. Oh, there were one-reel abridgements of *We Want*

Three "Ex-Stooges" pose with their environmentally friendly vacuuming contraption on location for *Kook's Tour* (Normandy Productions, 1970).
COURTESY OF C3 ENTERTAINMENT, INC.

Our Mummy and *Studio Stoops*, in "8mm Ultrasonic Sound." A murky, easily scratched Super 8 sound print of a Stooge two-reeler sold for about thirty smackers in 1975 dollars, so you youngsters who can effortlessly plop a ten-dollar DVD into the player and watch a whole festival of Stooge shorts from pristine 35mm source material — count your blessings.

Mike began running conventions for old movie buffs in the Orange County area so that we could buy stills, posters, films and other memorabilia without having to schlep all the way into Hollywood, which we still did anyway. Mike called these get-togethers "Casual Cons," and while I don't recall being conned by anyone at these affairs, I do remember the casual and good-natured atmosphere. On September 26, 1976, Mike hosted a Casual Con at a hotel in Anaheim, and the special guest was Joe DeRita.

For some reason, I didn't take my reel-to-reel tape recorder, but I did take my newly acquired Sankyo Super 8 sound movie camera and plenty of Kodak cartridges. The camera and a wonderful Elmo ST-1200 Super 8 sound projector were the gifts from my parents upon my graduation that past June from Western High School.

Thanks, Mom and Dad.

Joe wore a burgundy-colored polo shirt and a string tie with a western-style buckle on it. I'm not sure if he had shaved his head just for this event or if he'd taken to this hairstyle permanently after joining the Stooges, but he was instantly recognizable. He was quite a bit heavier than he'd been during his days with the Stooges, and it took him a while to hobble down the corridor to a coffee shop where we all had breakfast. His eyesight was not good, and he had a jeweler's loupe which he used for reading. I remember him very carefully scanning the menu before ordering his breakfast. While he did not eat a lot (surprisingly), he was very precise about the way he wanted the food prepared. This may have been for health reasons. I think he ordered scrambled eggs and toast, with no butter on the toast.

For most of the day, Joe sat at a table and was happy to autograph photos and chat with fans. Jeff, Greg and I sat with him all day and just talked with him about a variety of subjects. It was clear that he was a very intelligent man, with definite opinions on a wide variety of topics, which he expressed in mildly salty language. (I remember him speculating on the sexual orientation of one of the local television entertainment reporters.) Joe may have had to watch his diet, but he still enjoyed a long, expensive cigar — several of them, in fact, over the course of the afternoon we spent with him.

Joe mentioned the tie with the western buckle. "We each got one of these after we played the Calgary Stampede," he explained. "It's a huge Western festival and rodeo in Canada. And we played there and laid the biggest bomb in history!" We also talked about the *Three Stooges Songbook* album that he had made with Moe and Larry for Coral Records in 1959. "That's the one where we *tried* to sing," he cracked. It soon became apparent that Joe was frequently a harsh critic of his own work, and occasionally of Moe and Larry's abilities.

Joe was not only a very interesting conversationalist, he was also genuinely interested in other people. I remember him asking us questions about what we liked in movies, and my film of our meeting shows him listening intently as we talk to him. Greg related how his parents didn't want him or Jeff to watch the Stooges when they were very young, because they thought the films were too violent. "We had a portable TV in our room," Greg said, "and we used to crawl under our bed — we'd sneak under it and watch the Stooges anyway!"

Joe replied, "Well, there's a lot of controversy about the violence. But you see, at the time these were made for kids in theaters, not three-year-olds or four-year-olds. These were made for kids eight, nine, ten years old, and they knew better. But a lot of these people now sit their kids in front of the TV to get 'em off their back for a while. They don't care what they're watching. So a little kid sees something on the TV and turns around and pokes his kid sister in the eye! He don't know any better."

We talked about the quartet of two-reelers that Joe had made for Columbia before joining the Stooges: *Slappily Married* (1946), *The Good Bad Egg* (1947), *Wedlock Deadlock* (1947) and *Jitter Bughouse* (1948). He seemed to be recalling a scene in *Slappily Married* when he said, "The material I did in those things, you could have got a busboy to do. You know, you get hit in the head with an egg, and your wife leaves you, and you say, 'Wait, honey!' And that's it. You know, it wasn't my personality. That stuff worked for other guys, and Columbia made a lot of shorts like that."

Joe had been a top comedian with the Minsky's burlesque circuit, and had learned the whole catalogue of routines. He felt that very little of his comic ability got preserved on film. He was not only dissatisfied with the formulaic, by-the-numbers routines he'd had to do as a solo comic at Columbia, he was also frustrated that he couldn't inject some new life into the routines which the Stooges did in personal appearances. He said that he'd always gotten along well with Moe and Larry, and while they weren't particularly close socially, it was "a pleasant business association." But he did have one comment that would probably scorch the ears of many a Three Stooges fan — and I have it on film to prove it.

"I don't think the Three Stooges were funny!" Joe was emphatic about this, and pounded his fist on the table as he said again, "I don't think the Three Stooges were funny! They were physical — what made them good was what they did physically. But to be a comedian, you see, you have to have a comedic point of view — a, a humor! And neither one, Moe nor Larry, had any humor. They only knew what they had been doing for twenty-four years and continued to do it. And I would give them a new line, or some new jokes, and they would burn them alive, because they didn't know them — they'd never done them before."

Still, Joe did enjoy some of the Stooge films. "I think the best one was *Around the World in a Daze*," he stated, "because it had a good story line to begin with. And we merely, in our bungling way, copied the story line that was already established. But the most money we made was on *The Three Stooges Meet Hercules*. The reason for that was because two years before, Joseph Levine bought the American rights to the Italian *Hercules* movie with Steve Reeves, and then spent twice as much as the movie cost to make in publicity. So there was kind of a Hercules craze."

About the Stooges' last film, *Kook's Tour*, he said, "Well, the idea behind it was all right, but we couldn't do nothin' with it, we couldn't sell it."

Right around that time, however, Super 8 distributor Niles Films was selling color prints of the hour-long movie, a comedy travelogue. It's quite enjoyable; a lovely, relaxed finale to a forty-year film career for the Stooges.

Joe expressed his devotion to his wife, Jean. "She looks after me, and gets me everything I need. I still go out for some cigars at the market, and I look after the dogs, and I sit on my front porch — but I can't see the people across the street."

GOD BLESS ALL CLOWNS

I was blessed to fall in love with movie comedy at a very early age, thanks to the Stooges. In my teens and twenties I was able to interview dozens of people who'd worked in the comedy factories of the 1920s, '30s and '40s — people who would be gone just a few years later. I treasure my memories of meeting Larry Fine and Joe DeRita, and of my many visits with Joe Besser. And I'll never forget the wonderful and high-spirited times I shared with the young stooges who introduced me to the real Stooges — John Cawley, and Jeff and Greg Lenburg. Thanks forever, guys. You're my favorite lame-brains.

RANDY SKRETVEDT IS THE AUTHOR OF *LAUREL & HARDY: THE MAGIC BEHIND THE MOVIES*. HE HAS INTERVIEWED MORE THAN 200 VETERANS OF THE GOLDEN AGE OF MOVIES AND OLD-TIME RADIO. FOR NINE YEARS HE WROTE AND EDITED *PAST TIMES*, A MAGAZINE ABOUT VINTAGE ENTERTAINMENT, AND HE TAUGHT A FILM HISTORY CLASS FOR FOUR YEARS. HE HAS PROVIDED COMMENTARY FOR A NUMBER OF DVDS, AND HAS WRITTEN BOOKLET NOTES FOR 25 COMPACT DISCS OF 1920S AND '30S MUSIC. HIS COLLECTION OF MORE THAN 30,000 RECORDS FORMS THE BASIS OF HIS WEEKLY RADIO SHOW, *FORWARD INTO THE PAST*, HEARD EACH SUNDAY AFTERNOON FOR MORE THAN 25 YEARS OVER KSPC-FM 88.7 IN THE LOS ANGELES AREA (AND WORLDWIDE THROUGH WWW.KSPC.ORG). HE CAN ALSO BE HEARD IN A VARIETY OF SILLY VOICES ON *THE SUNSET REVIEW*, A COMEDY PROGRAM ON KSPC.

A Star Is Born

by Gary Owens

It was a hot summer day in 1983. Bearing up under the blazing sun was the biggest gathering in the history of the Hollywood Walk of Fame — seven thousand in all. They had begun arriving as early as seven o'clock that morning. By afternoon the crowd covered four blocks, from Sunset Boulevard to Selma Avenue. Many of these dedicated individuals had flown in from other countries. They were there for one purpose: to witness the unveiling of a star at 1560 Vine Street, bearing the name of the Three Stooges.

Of course, by this time Moe Howard, Larry Fine, Shemp Howard and Curly Howard were gone. Joe DeRita was not up to attending, but Joe Besser was there. So, too, was longtime foil Emil Sitka, and some co-stars from the Stooges' final theatrical feature, *The Outlaws Is Coming!* — Adam West, Jamie Farr and Henry Gibson. The Stooges' relatives were there as well. Covering the event were reporters from every major television network and newspaper. Milton Berle — who was one of the first stars to feature the trio on television — took the microphone and paid homage to the recipients of the star and mentioned the host of the event: "I've known the Three Stooges and Gary Owens for many, many years. This wonderful tribute to the Stooges is both fitting and proper — which is more than I can say about Gary Owens' suit."

That was typical Milton. He was a good friend of mine. I've been in show business for fifty years and have known and worked with over 2,000 celebrities, including the Three Stooges.

COURTESY OF GARY OWENS.

LOVE AT FIRST BITE

My first exposure to the zany trio came when I was growing up in Plankinton, South Dakota. Plankinton (Population: 600) had only one movie theater — the Anjune — and it was there that I was introduced to the comedy of Moe, Larry and Curly. I became such a fan that I wanted to pattern my whole life after them. I would like to have worked as the chief anesthesiologist at the Three Stooges Hospital, knocking patients out with a frying pan. But instead I went into radio. My first job was as the news director for a little station called KORN (Those were the actual call letters). I was sixteen years old at the time. Before long, I was working as a newscaster on network television and radio. Later, when I moved to Nebraska, I got a job at KOIL Omaha. As fate would have it, the morning disc jockey became angry with the owner of the station and quit right in the middle of his show. The only other employees in the building were the chief engineer and me, so I stepped in. That was my

Gary and the Boys at a Hollywood premiere, circa 1959.

first DJ job, and frankly, I was semi-terrible. But I kept at it, and within two months' time, my show was number one in the city. Listeners must have been dialing in to see what else could go wrong.

When I was twenty I moved to Hollywood and began to meet the stars I had watched from the balcony of the Anjune Theater. I first came face to face with the Three Stooges sometime in the late fifties at a movie premiere I was hosting. Off camera, Moe and Larry were very different from their screen characters; both men were quiet and serious. Moe, in fact, was a Shakespearean scholar. Over time I became quite friendly with both him and Larry — and Joe Besser as well. We occasionally had lunch together (although not at the same time) at the Smoke House Restaurant in "Beautiful Downtown Burbank." After Larry had his stroke, I would visit him at the Motion Picture Country Home in Woodland Hills.

THE PEST MAN WINS

When I was elected to the Board of the Hollywood Chamber of Commerce in 1983, I received a list of the 1500 or so individuals who had a star on the legendary Walk of Fame. Half-jokingly, I asked the Chamber's then-President Bill Welsh, the Vice-President, Bill Hertz and Hollywood's Honorary Mayor Johnny Grant, "Where's the star for the Three Stooges?"

They didn't know; they had presumed that the veteran comics had one, however. Certainly they deserved one, they all agreed.

The fact that the Stooges had no star was a bone of contention for the comics. They had even thought of taking matters into their own hands and rectifying this oversight. According to *The Three Stooges Scrapbook*: "In 1964 Moe, Larry and Curly-Joe came up with the clever idea of painting a huge gold star, at midnight, in the center of the intersection of Hollywood and Vine. The boys planned to dress up in painter's overalls, block off the street and paint their names inside a gigantic mock-up of the star. Moe abandoned the midnight escapade at the last minute, evidently fearing the police might arrest them."

Moe and Larry were probably used to being treated poorly by those in the industry. I don't think that Harry Cohn even let them eat in the Columbia commissary! But the fact that they had not received a star on the Hollywood Walk of Fame . . . *That* was too much for me.

At the time I was doing a national radio show heard in 250 cities. "Let me nominate them through my station," I said. "And I'll pay for the star myself."

I went to see the manager of KIIS, Wally Clark, and said, "I want to sponsor the Three Stooges; will you folks help me out?"

At that time there was a fee of $3,000 for a star. But paying that fee does not necessarily ensure that your nominee will receive one. That decision ultimately rests with the twelve members who make up the nominating committee — and their finding must be unanimous. I began to travel the country, eliciting the support of prominent writers from television, radio and newspapers. (Jeff and Greg Lenburg, the co-authors of *The Three Stooges Scrapbook*, were of tremendous assistance to me throughout this process.) We received something like 40,000 letters from around the world, each one stating that the Three Stooges should be added to the Hollywood Walk of Fame.

And on August 30, 1983, they were. I was proud to serve as emcee for that wonderful event.

In the years since, I have continued to champion my favorite comedy trio. I have hosted various events related to the Stooges, including a retrospective on the TV Land network and the dedication ceremony of the Jules White Wall at the Motion Picture Home. And I was presented with the Knucklehead Appreciation Award at the First Annual West Coast Stooge Convention. That event was recorded for posterity and can be seen on the Anchor Bay DVD, *The Three Stooges All-Time Favorites.*

The Stooges have become something of a personal crusade for me.

I love them.

GARY OWENS IS BEST KNOWN AS THE ANNOUNCER ON *ROWAN AND MARTIN'S LAUGH-IN.* HE HAS ALSO LENT HIS FAMILIAR BARITONE VOICE TO SOME 3,000 CARTOONS, 35,000 COMMERCIALS AND SIXTEEN TELEVISION SERIES. HE CAN STILL BE HEARD DAILY ON HIS OWN NETWORK RADIO PROGRAM. GARY WAS INDUCTED INTO THE NATIONAL RADIO HALL OF FAME IN 1994 (ALONGSIDE FELLOW RECIPIENTS GEORGE BURNS, RED SKELTON AND GARRISON KEILLOR) AND THE NATIONAL TELEVISION HALL OF FAME IN 2002. HIS OWN HOLLYWOOD WALK OF FAME STAR (IN RECOGNITION OF HIS RADIO WORK) IS LOCATED AT 6743 HOLLYWOOD BOULEVARD; HE IS SCHEDULED TO RECEIVE A SECOND ONE (THIS TIME FOR HIS TELEVISION CAREER) IN 2008.

ALL THE WORLD'S A STOOGE

BY GARY LASSIN

As a child in the early 1960s, there were two parts to every day: school and after-school. For me, school meant "the three R's," while after-school meant The Three Stooges.

Back then, there were only three TV channels, so when the Stooges came on they occupied fully one-third of the airwaves. Because of this, every kid in town knew and loved the Stooges. And why not? Their mayhem and fast-paced antics provided an escape from the drudgery of addition, subtraction, Dick & Jane primers and practice runs to the basement fallout shelter.

As human cartoons, the Stooges got in and out of ridiculous situations, just like the animated cartoon characters did. But the fact that they were real people set them apart from all the other cartoons. While it might have been amusing to see a talking rabbit try and plug up an oil geyser by sitting on it, seeing Curly Howard try the same thing was downright hysterical. Even as a young kid I could see that while *Popeye* was okay and *The Roadrunner* was pretty good, it was the Stooges who were #1.

Fast-forward to the late 1970s. I'm now a grad student and I'm out on a first date with a girl named Robin Solomon who tells me that she's related to somebody famous. I couldn't think of any famous Solomons. Who could it be, I wondered John Lennon? Chevy Chase? Marlon Brando? Nah, it had to be somebody totally uncool like Lawrence Welk or Perry Como. Anyway, after much hemming and hawing, it was apparent that she was reluctant to "spill the beans," not being overly proud of her famous relative and thinking his name would be a turn-off, especially on a first date. After much cajoling however, the truth is finally revealed . . . she's related to (gulp), Larry of The Three Stooges.

SAVED BY THE BELLE

Life-changing moments don't happen every day, but it was right then and there that I realized I had to figure out a way to get this girl to marry me. After all, I had dated girls who were smart, girls who were beautiful and girls who were witty conversationalists. But when would I ever find another girl related to a Stooge!

As our relationship got more serious she invited me to visit her grandfather, Morris "Moe" Feinberg, who was Larry Fine's younger brother. How ironic that Larry's brother was known as Moe! Although Larry had died several years earlier, Moe's voice and his mannerisms clearly smacked of his brother Larry. He told me countless stories about his brother and that for years he had even been working on a book about him, to be titled *My Brother Was a Movie Star*. While I hated the title, I loved the stories. Moe told them with a warmth and passion that made his love and admiration for his brother readily apparent. He would slip into Jewish dialect

"Uncle Max" pays a visit. Robin Solomon, her sister Joy and their two cousins Andy and Bob Aerenson pose with their famous relative. Wilmington, Delaware, December 1968. COURTESY OF GARY LASSIN

Morris "Moe" Feinberg demonstrates his dance moves at Gary and Robin Lassin's wedding reception at the Hotel Dupont, Wilmington, Delaware; June 7, 1981. COURTESY OF GARY LASSIN

when a story called for it, or even do a little soft-shoe tap dancing to help illustrate one of the old routines. And I was really impressed that a man in his late seventies, with a heart condition, was not only running a Three Stooges Fan Club and publishing a bi-monthly newsletter, but also had the energy and desire to publish a book.

Eventually, Robin and I did indeed get married and I was now part of Larry Fine's family. Moe and I became very close for several reasons. First off, I was the only one in the family that had any interest at all in his Stooges stuff. While not a collector, Moe enjoyed showing off the few pieces that he owned, the letters he had received from Larry and the family photos from the old days. And I was the only person who enjoyed seeing it all. But more importantly, I soon became the son/grandson that he never had. Moe had two daughters and five granddaughters, but no sons or grandsons. My own grandfathers were both dead at this point, so Moe and I bonded quite closely and he inspired me to start collecting Stooges memorabilia on my own.

I soon learned that collecting the Stooges was a wonderful hobby. Unlike collecting stamps, coins or baseball cards in which the objects are all pretty much the same, Stooges memorabilia cut across many different collecting fields. I was soon accumulating toys & games, posters, news clippings, autographs, photos, playbills, and even sheet music. The diversity and breadth of material available on the Stooges was unbelievable and I was hooked.

Anyway, despite his failing health, Moe finally found a publisher for his book (which fortunately was retitled, *Larry, the Stooge in the Middle*) and it was the crowning achievement in his life. He became somewhat of a celebrity in his own right, doing interviews with radio stations around the country and making personal appearances to promote and autograph the book.

Sadly, Moe passed away soon after. But it was truly a gift from above that his failing heart had somehow held out long enough to see his efforts come to fruition.

PASSING THE TORCH

Shortly after Moe's death in May 1986, I began to rummage through the stacks of unanswered Stooges mail that he had received. I just assumed that Moe's death meant the death of the Stooges fan club as well, since it was basically a one-man operation and that one man was no longer around. But reading through this

IS AN OFFICIAL MEMBER IN GOOD STANDING

DATE　　　　　PRESIDENT

COURTESY OF GARY LASSIN

mail I had an epiphany. Fan after fan seemed to echo the same few familiar sentiments, which were basically:

1) "I've loved the Stooges ever since I can remember."
2) "My mailbox is always full with bills and junk mail, but your newsletter is the only piece of mail I really look forward to receiving."

This was the first time I really got a taste of how deeply passionate the Stooges' fans were. And after reading these letters, there was no way I was going to let the club die a natural death. I had to try and keep it alive if at all possible.

I had no idea how to run a fan club or what was involved. And how would I get material for a newsletter? After all, the original Stooges were long-dead and not making any new films. What could I possibly write about issue after issue?

I decided to seek help from a fellow named Paul Wesolowski. Paul was running a Marx Brothers fan club (which he dubbed *The Marx Brotherhood*) and he lived only about thirty minutes away from me. He graciously invited me out to his place to talk and give me some pointers.

When I arrived at his townhouse, I was completely blown away. The guy was residing in a veritable Marx Brothers museum! The walls were covered with posters, photos and all sorts of rare memorabilia. He was eating off of Marx Brothers dishes and being awakened by a Marx Brothers alarm clock. Every square inch had a Marxist theme to it.

While Paul did have a few good ideas, what I really took away most from that meeting was: *SOME DAY I'VE GOTTA HAVE A STOOGES PLACE LIKE THAT!*

There was only one catch: Paul Wesolowski was a single guy with no wifely "boss" telling him how he could or couldn't decorate his place. Meanwhile, I was stuck with Robin Solomon Lassin. You remember her. That girl that got me started down this slippery Stooges slope to begin with.

It turns out that when Robin was a child, she was deathly afraid of the Stooges. She didn't like all the slaps, pokes and head-bonks (in other words, all the *good stuff*). In fact, whenever she heard that her Uncle Larry was coming to visit she would get terribly upset and fearful. To calm her fears, her parents started to refer to him as "Uncle Max" instead. Somehow this ruse worked and she was never fearful when Uncle Max came to visit. But clearly, this was no Stooges fan that I married. And there was no way, no how, that the walls of our home were going to be plastered with Stoogeabilia.

Anyway, I tucked away my fantasy for the time being and I announced to the fan club members that I was going to try to keep the club going. At that point, an amazing thing happened. The members rallied around me much like a football team does when the starting quarterback goes down and the second stringer must lead the team. They sent in all kinds of articles, news clippings and photos for the newsletter. They sent letters of encouragement and offered to help in any way they possibly could, even if it was just to lend moral support.

Before long, I had a backlog of material for the newsletter and we began having annual conventions so that fans could get together and share their common bond. The conventions were hugely successful and garnered national attention in newspapers and magazines as well as on TV and radio. This further fueled the growth of the fan club and interest in the Stooges.

CROSSROADS

As the years went by, my Stooges collection continued to grow by leaps and bounds. I picked up items from every conceivable source: Stooges relatives, other collectors, flea markets and antique shows, magazine ads, and eventually, the Internet. Unfortunately it was all being filed away in boxes, drawers, binders and filing cabinets.

This was becoming increasingly frustrating because I couldn't really enjoy my own collection, but also because I couldn't share all this great stuff I had amassed with other fans and collectors.

Everything changed in March 2000. My wife became ill and the doctors were at a loss to explain her symptoms. Initially they thought she might have hepatitis, and then they suspected it might be gallstones. Finally they determined that a malignant tumor was the culprit . . . a tumor which needed to be removed with one of the most lengthy & complex general surgical procedures that can be performed, called a "Whipple Resection." It's an operation which is rarely performed and one in which a full ten percent of patients do not survive the procedure itself.

Fortunately, my wife made it through the surgery and made a spectacular recovery. She's now seven years post-op and cancer free.

But this chain of events made me start thinking about my own mortality and what if our positions had been reversed. What would I really regret not having done with my life if all of a sudden my number was called?

The answer was clear and I knew what I had to do. It was time for the Stooges to have their museum.

As soon as my wife was recovered and back to her old self, I began work on the project. I located and purchased a building (in Spring House, Pennsylvania) that I thought would make a suitable home for my stuff, and I engaged a museum design firm to assist me in how to best utilize the space and to help me in conceptualizing, planning and designing the layout of the exhibits.

BEDLAM IN PARADISE

For most of the next three years, we worked together on the project, constantly designing, refining and redesigning. Several thousand items had to be measured and photographed so that exhibit cases and displays could be laid out. Copy had to be written to describe the items. The process was quite involved because I knew nothing about building a museum, while the museum planners knew nothing about the Stooges. They would lay out a minor Joe DeRita piece right at eye level and put Larry Fine's driver's license, one of my best pieces, way down at the bottom of a case. Since the pieces were different sizes and couldn't just be flip-flopped, I'd have to get the entire case redesigned. Then I'd wind up purchasing a new Joe DeRita item that was better than the one in the existing layout . . . and so again they'd have to redesign that case. This went on and on for quite some time.

One thing I knew for sure was that I wanted the "Stooges experience" to begin as soon as a visitor walked through the front door. What better way to accomplish this than to have the Stooges' familiar "Hello"

"Hello"

"Hello"

ring out in unison when a fan entered the building? This seemed simple enough but it actually turned out to be quite complicated to pull off. The greeting couldn't merely be triggered by the opening of the front door because it wouldn't make sense to hear this upon leaving the building, only upon entering. So my consultants rigged up a series of motion sensors, which needed to be tripped just *after* the opening of the door, for the greeting to be heard. If the sensors were tripped just *before* the door was opened, we knew that was someone leaving the building and the greeting would not sound.

Organizing my diverse collection of artifacts into visitor-friendly, themed sections was also a daunting challenge. A narrow corridor on the ground level would become *Lobby Card Lane*, a home to the 11x14 posters that once adorned the theater lobbies. An area devoted to foreign Stooges posters would be named *All the World's A Stooge*. Photos of fanatical fans with their Stooges tattoos, customized vans, etc. would be placed in an area called

The Stoogeum under construction. Spring House, Pennsylvania, 2002.
COURTESY OF GARY LASSIN

Stooge-a-holics Unanimous. The third floor art gallery would feature subsections for animation cels (*Howard and Fine Art*) and pencil drawings (*Pop Goes the Easel*).

Areas were also carved out for trade ads (*Tricks of the Trade*) and for toys, games and novelties (*Mass Marketed Morons*). Each Stooge would get his own life-size cutout, behind which would be a case housing personal belongings and memorabilia related to that Stooge.

For the 85-seat *Stoogeum Theater*, lining the walls with some extremely rare Stooges one-sheet movie posters from the 1930s seemed like just the right touch.

Sometimes, inspiration came from unlikely sources. While lunching in a New York City deli, I noticed their wall of autographed photos of the celebrities that had eaten there. From that visit, the Stoogeum's *Deli Wall* was born, an entire wall of autographed photos of the Stooges' supporting players.

On and on this process went until everything had an appropriate home.

It was during this period that I began to try to think of a name for the place. I wanted to come up with something catchy, not simply "The Three Stooges Museum." I brainstormed for quite awhile, rejecting names such as "Stoogeway to Heaven," "Stoogeworld USA" and a myriad of other losers. Finally, I began looking long and hard at the words "Stooges" and "Museum." Somehow, my mind began fusing the two words together, and then it hit me . . . the building needed to be called "The Stoogeum."

Also during this design period, I began to formulate the Stoogeum's *raison d'être*. I soon had the following mission statement in mind:

> *To collect, preserve and interpret historically or culturally*
> *significant pieces of Stoogeabilia in order to further the*
> *public's enjoyment and appreciation of The Three Stooges and to*
> *maintain the legacy of their comedy for future generations.*

I wanted The Stoogeum to be a place that:
a) The Boys would be honored and proud to be associated with if they were alive today.
b) A die-hard Stooges fan would like to have his ashes scattered over.

OIL'S WELL THAT ENDS WELL

In the spring of 2004, The Stoogeum finally had its grand opening. While I always expected that the Stoogeum would be a popular destination for hard-core fans, surprisingly, there has also been a great deal of interest from groups that are not specifically Stooge aficionados. I've had a steady steam of church groups, antique clubs, cinephile organizations, rotary clubs and others as visitors. In addition, the building has proven to be a popular venue for fundraising events for organizations such as the Philadelphia Ronald McDonald House and others. In fact, I received so many requests for more information about the building that I had to put up a website (www.stoogeum.com) to handle all the inquiries.

The Completed Stoogeum. February 2004. COURTESY OF GARY LASSIN

One of the many displays in the Stoogeum: Pictured are the jackets Moe, Larry and Curly-Joe wore in their stage act in the late sixties, along with rare publicity stills and posters. COURTESY OF GARY LASSIN

In the tradition of Moe Feinberg, I'm basically a one-man operation. For now, the building does not have regular operating hours; it is open by appointment only. But in order to reach as wide an audience as possible, I've made it a policy not to charge any admission fee to see the collection.

New items and exhibits are constantly being added. In 2008, visitors can now enjoy the *Hall of Shemp* (anything and everything Shemp), *Stoogeology 101* (a primer in Stooge history for the uninitiated), as well as *The Making of the Stoogeum*, an area which tells the story behind the Stoogeum.

Because of the unique nature of the Stoogeum, it has generated a great deal of interest from the press. I've had a nonstop barrage of requests for interviews from newspapers as well as radio & TV stations, gaining a fair amount of local notoriety for myself and for the building.

In fact, all the hoopla surrounding the Stoogeum has even changed my wife's attitude towards the Stooges. Nowadays, when she tells someone that she is related to somebody famous and they ask who it is, she proudly replies, "The Curator of the Stoogeum"!

GARY LASSIN IS A LIFELONG THREE STOOGES FAN WHO GREW UP IN THE PHILADELPHIA AREA. HE RECEIVED A B.A. IN ECONOMICS AND POLITICAL SCIENCE FROM BRANDEIS UNIVERSITY AND AN M.B.A. FROM THE UNIVERSITY OF PENNSYLVANIA'S WHARTON SCHOOL. HE IS ALSO A CPA (INACTIVE) IN THE STATE OF PENNSYLVANIA. AS THE THREE STOOGES FAN CLUB PRESIDENT, CURATOR OF *THE STOOGEUM* AND A MEMBER OF LARRY FINE'S FAMILY, GARY HAS DONE COUNTLESS RADIO & TV INTERVIEWS AND CAN BE SEEN IN PROGRAMS SUCH AS A&E'S *BIOGRAPHY*. IN "REAL LIFE," GARY IS EMPLOYED AS THE VICE-PRESIDENT OF FINANCE FOR A NATIONAL DIRECT-MAIL CATALOG COMPANY. FOR MORE INFORMATION, CLICK ON WWW.STOOGEUM.COM AND WWW.THREESTOOGES.NET.

Original drawing by Gary Owens

AFTERWORD

It all seems like a dream now. Did we *really* come to know the Stooges — not just as movie icons, but as personal friends and mentors? The answer, of course, is yes, but it still seems a distant connection. We have all aged in the years since the original members of the team left us, but — thanks to film preservation — their performances on celluloid remain as fresh and sparkling as they did when they were new. Many of these black-and-white films have been digitally restored, and can now be seen in what appears to be authentic color.

The Stooges themselves might be surprised to know that their unsophisticated brand of humor would flourish in the twenty-first century. They were not geniuses after all, nor did they ever pretend to be. They were simply hardworking vaudevillians and seasoned clowns, grateful for the opportunity to earn their living by making audiences laugh. They could never have envisioned that teenagers in the distant future would be walking around with something called an iPhone, with a tiny image of a film they made as far back as 1934.

It is safe to assume, however, that Moe Howard, Larry Fine, Curly Howard, Shemp Howard, Joe Besser and Joe DeRita would be pleased to see their influence on the major comedy stars of today. They would be honored by their star on the Hollywood Walk of Fame, and be rendered speechless by a tour of the Stoogeum.

Just as we lament that times have changed, that nothing makes us laugh anymore, that the Stooges are gone, we watch the familiar scenes of three grown men acting like children, and we — and they — are young again.

SUGGESTED STOOGE READING

Besser, Joe with Jeff and Greg Lenburg. *Not Just a Stooge: The Autobiography of Hollywood's Most Prolific Third Stooge* (with a foreword by Milton Berle). Excelsior Books, 1984. (Revised and reissued as *Once a Stooge, Always a Stooge* in 1988 and 1990.) A sentimental memoir, *Not Just a Stooge* embodies the chubby comic's remarkable career, from his stint as a magician's assistant in vaudeville, to his frequent appearances on stage, screen, radio and television.

Bruskin, David N. *The White Brothers: Jack, Jules and Sam White.* The Directors Guild of America, 1993; reissued as *Behind the Three Stooges: The White Brothers.* This collection of interviews with the men who oversaw the majority of the Stooges' two-reel product should be required reading for the serious Stooge buff.

Cox, Steve and Jim Terry. *One Fine Stooge: Larry Fine's Frizzy Life in Pictures.* Cumberland Press, 2006. This colorful coffee-table style book is everything Larry would have liked his biography *Stroke of Luck* to be. Profusely illustrated with rare photographs and drawings, it offers an affectionate look at the "Stooge in the Middle."

Epstein, Lawrence J. *Mixed Nuts: America's Love Affair with Comedy Teams: From Burns and Allen to Belushi and Aykroyd.* Public Affairs, 2004. This examination of American comedy covers a wide span, from nineteenth-century vaudeville to silent movies to talkies to television sitcoms. The Three Stooges, of course, figure prominently into the equation.

Feinberg, Moe. *Larry, The Stooge in the Middle* (with a foreword by Steve Allen). Last Gasp of San Francisco, 1984. This is a chronological look at the life of Larry Fine, written by his older brother. Morris Feinberg (known as "Moe") published *The Three Stooges Journal* from his home in Philadelphia, Pennsylvania. When he died in 1986, the club and the *Journal* were revamped by Morris's grandson-in-law, Gary Lassin.

Flannagan, Bill. *Last of the Moe Haircuts: The Influence of the Three Stooges on Twentieth Century Culture.* Contemporary Books, 1986. In the words of one reviewer: "The time has come to reveal what we have all somehow sensed — That the only logical explanation for the Twentieth Century world of ours is . . . The Three Stooges."

Fleming, Michael. *The Three Stooges: An Illustrated History, From Amalgamated Morons to American Icons.* Doubleday & Co., 1999 (paperback reprint, Broadway Books, 2002). This combination biography/filmography offers high-resolution scene stills from the

Columbia shorts. Each short is rated according to the number of slaps and pokes that Larry, Curly or Shemp endured during each twenty-minute outing. This also was credited as the source for the ABC TV movie *The Three Stooges*, produced by actor/director Mel Gibson (who supplied the book's foreword).

Forrester, Jeffrey. *The Stooge Chronicles*. Contemporary Books, 1981. This large-size paperback book offered a fresh look at the Stooges' history, with an emphasis on the contribution of the team's longtime co-star, Emil Sitka. There are also several quotes and photographs of Paul "Mousie" Garner, one of Ted Healy's replacement Stooges; he also claimed to have been a contender for the Third Stooge spot vacated by Curly and Shemp. All in all, the book is well done, with some interesting photos of the team throughout their fifty-year career.

Forrester, Jeff, with Tom Forrester and Joe Wallison. *The Three Stooges: The Triumphs and Tragedies of the Most Popular Comedy Team of All Time*. Donaldson Books, 2005. This well-received book examines the careers not only of Moe, Larry, Curly and Shemp, but of Ted Healy's other stooges as well, including Paul "Mousie" Garner (who provided the foreword).

Forrester, Tom. *The Stooges' Lost Episodes*. Contemporary Books, 1988. This paperback volume "is intended as a guidebook to assist Stoogemaniacs in getting their hands on the 'lost' stuff that is now available. In addition, the authors have included a filmography that lists the lost episodes of the Three Stooges — both collectively and individually."

Garner, Paul. *Mousie Garner: Autobiography of a Vaudeville Stooge*. McFarland & Co., 1999. Paul Garner (1909-2004) was one of more than twenty comics who supported Ted Healy in the 1930s. In the mid-1970s he and Curly-Joe DeRita formed an unsuccessful act called The New Three Stooges. Garner outlived all of his contemporaries, and was occasionally called upon to give his impressions of the legendary comedy team. Steve Allen provided the foreword.

Howard, Moe. *Moe Howard and the 3 Stooges: The Pictorial Biography of the Wildest Trio in the History of American Entertainment.* Citadel Press, 1977. Moe penned this autobiography himself under the working title, "I Stooge to Conquer." After his death in 1975, his daughter Joan and her husband Norman Maurer (who wrote the Afterword) saw to it that the book was published. Their efforts were greatly appreciated by Stooge fans. The book was reissued time and again.

Kurson, Robert. *The Official Three Stooges Encyclopedia: The Ultimate Knucklehead's Guide to Stoogedom, from Amalgamated Morons to Ziller, Zeller, and Zoller.* Contemporary Books, 1998. This oversized book contains an alphabetical listing of catch phrases and routines associated with the team.

Lenburg, Jeff with Joan Howard Maurer and Greg Lenburg. *The Three Stooges Scrapbook.* The Citadel Press, 1982; reprinted in 1994. Originally published in hardback, *The Three Stooges Scrapbook* contains chapters on the team's historical overview, merchandise, comic books, television appearances, audio recordings, impersonators, and their massive fan base. It also offers an exemplary filmography, as well as insightful profiles on the team, beginning with the Stooges' founder, Ted Healy. Joe Besser supplied the foreword.

Maltin, Leonard. *Movie Comedy Teams.* Signet Books, 1970; revised and reprinted in 1974 and 1985. This groundbreaking paperback book featured such acclaimed partnerships as Laurel and Hardy, Abbott and Costello, the Marx Brothers, and offered — for the first time ever — a chapter-length overview of the Stooges and their film legacy.

— *The Great Movie Comedians: From Charlie Chaplin to Woody Allen.* Crown Publishers, 1978. Leonard Maltin was inspired to write this book after attending the eight-month Bicentennial Salute to American Film Comedy at the Museum of Modern Art in New York City. The result is a fresh appraisal of such funnymen as Laurel and Hardy, W.C. Fields, Will Rogers, and, of course, the Three Stooges.

— *The Great Movie Shorts: Those Wonderful One-and-Two-Reelers of the Thirties and Forties*. Crown Books, 1972; reissued as *Selected Short Subjects: From Spanky to the Three Stooges* by DaCapo Books in 1983. This compendium of essays and filmographies chronicles the careers of such comedy favorites as Our Gang, Laurel and Hardy, Robert Benchley, Harry Langdon, Andy Clyde, Charley Chase and Leon Errol. As in his previous work *Movie Comedy Teams*, Leonard Maltin gives the Stooges their proper due.

Maurer, Joan Howard. *Curly: An Illustrated Biography of the Superstooge* (with a foreword by Michael Jackson). The Citadel Press, 1985 (reissued in paperback). This fascinating look at everyone's favorite Third Stooge was written by Curly Howard's niece.

— *The Three Stooges Book of Scripts*. The Citadel Press, 1984. A hardback containing reprints of the actual scripts from three popular two-reelers: *Men in Black* (1934), *Three Little Pigskins* (1934) and *You Nazty Spy* (1940). The book also contains frame blowups from each film, along with production notes.

— *The Three Stooges Book of Scripts II*. The Citadel Press, 1987. The first book of scripts apparently sold very well, warranting a second volume. This release featured *Restless Knights* (1935), *We Want Our Mummy* (1939) and *Yes, We Have No Bonanza* (1939). There is also a chapter devoted to the 1962 Columbia feature, *The Three Stooges Meet Hercules*.

Okuda, Ted with Edward Watz. *The Columbia Comedy Shorts: Two-Reel Hollywood Film Comedies, 1933-1958*. McFarland & Co., 1986 (softcover reprint, 1998). Film historians Ted Okuda and Edward Watz have written an outstanding history on the Columbia short subjects department, which produced 190 Stooge shorts during a continuous twenty-four year period. A number of surviving co-stars and directors contributed to this book, including Emil Sitka (who provided the foreword), Edward Bernds, Jules and Jack White and Elwood Ullman. It is dedicated to the Stooges' favorite foil, Vernon Dent.

Seely, Peter and Gail W. Pieper (editors). *Stoogeology: Essays on the Three Stooges.* McFarland & Co., 2007. This 272-page softcover book is a collection of nineteen scholarly essays about the Stooges, written primarily by college professors and academicians. Peter Seely, Professor of Communication Arts at Benedictine University (and member of the Three Stooges Fan Club), selected the following essays for this study: "The Aesthetics of Stooge Filmmaking," "Stooge Psychology and Religion," "The Stooges Go to War," and "Race, Ethnicity and Gender in Stooge Films."

Solomon, Jon. *The Complete Three Stooges: The Official Filmography and Three Stooges Companion.* Comedy III Productions, 2002. In his review of this authorized volume, Eric Lamond (Larry Fine's grandson), states: "Having intimate knowledge of the Three Stooges both personally and professionally, I was pleasantly surprised at the accuracy and detail brought to this filmography by Dr. Solomon . . . This book belongs in the library of every Three Stooges fan, comedy fan and film fan."